Heated Blues

Heated Blues

Observations on Loss and Longing

DEL LOUIS

Order this book online at www.trafford.com
or email orders@trafford.com

Most Trafford titles are also available at major online book retailers.

Printed in the United States of America.

ISBN: 978-1-4269-7293-5 (sc)
ISBN: 978-1-4269-7294-2 (hc)
ISBN: 978-1-4269-7295-9 (e)

Library of Congress Control Number: 2011910778

Trafford rev. 07/11/2011

 www.trafford.com

North America & International
toll-free: 1 888 232 4444 (USA & Canada)
phone: 250 383 6864 ♦ fax: 812 355 4082

Acknowledgements

To all those who helped carve, curve these ideas for this book. God knows I meander. Sometimes I've felt like someone else is the voice in my writing I'm just pushing the pen. Here are the ones I give tremendous thanks to. We all joined together through observation, landscapes, friends, acquaintances. Without them none of this is faintly possible: Don Yanchochik, Cathy Diehl, Emily Labelle, Hunter S. Thompson, of course Emily Carette; where are you hiding fav bartender, a waiter named Alison. Customer Dana for inspiration, to all the bartenders names Jen or Jenn, and the one "outback", Joan (my)first. M. Chaban, Eliz. Lesser, the girl from (RACC) who worked at Troopers, is it Sarah or Sara, you (twin). Angela, Charley, Heather, Sara did I spell that right, see you soon, the living God, Scott for pushing me further. And Bradley Cooper, trying to be as cool as he naturally. 'Nina' of "Brewers", we need another talk.

Customer Lenn who I miss after her birthday about 5 years ago. In truth, the theory is there is no theory that works, just try walking first. And be as honest as all my heroes especially Keith Richards. Also the divine inspiration of reading the works of Tim Carroll, Maggie Estep.

Preface

Del's reflective and insightful poems of general observations of realisms, truths, dreams still is from a period of longing of about 6-7 years. To feel and to reach out uncovering the soul, the fragments and frailty of living,

He hopes to take the readers on a loving but sad journey through one year of these feelings, filled with passion and loss as someone who's facing his own morality, limitations, hoping something is saved from immortality. He makes this project a volume 1 for those who like to read and think along the way. And also the searching, reaching for the illimitable or just something good.

"Why" (Pt. 2)

Why or when I try to enrage you
In anything even frivolous talk nothing works
You condemn my few friends but some people can't help their
Inclination and tendencies toward others to find the soul's place
The cost and the risks of breaking free of mores

And the scent on those thrown down keys could make me mad
And still I try to engage you in some ritualistic cultures
Whilst you said he is a stealer of someone's heart who displaced
    you
This hoodlum is not as bad as you personally he even has good
    points
But what do you do when time sheds wounds and darkness with
    an unknown message only Cassidy would know
Everything became catastrophic just think of any underlying
    message (saved)
In someone's quilt aura like looking at an antique lights sheen

She has nameless, endless plans as her beauty swells
Setting aside this man whose striped heart floats just above
A wrinkled wave the one that swirls and with us no emotion
    hiding below a star
Making me wonder why

"Moments like these"

Has the world so destructed from what the Kennedy's or our
   forefathers wished was something more
But were still divided or am I just feeling my own decimation
   and decay
Aid a God create all that's problematic a sheen so false and
   homicidal
Or wasn't primarily capitalism and wasteful gov't spending

I'm inclined to think we've all stopped short of being
   kissed-goodbye
As we wait for some kind of enlightenment above mankind
Mine might've been those casual encounters in squat haunts with
   ghosts,
But Dianna passed

You know some were real and wore inanely sweat shirts over got
   skin waiting on timed lovers
No one tells you all loss is inherit as nature or your captivating
   mush
And I can't tell you everything if I want to stop short of my own
   immortality
I must die like friends in airplanes over my head and nearby

While I'll just wait on this ancient copplestone corner
For that beauty with raven hair where these steps looked like red
   potatoes someone furnished
As the stars stare down I kind of like old city
And isn't it a pity when what you want leaves you
To a whiskey and it's rye I blend with the caramel flavor of coke
When I couldn't combine my arm to your hem your eyes bordered
   all my play
As I stare at your yoke colored hair

"Dazzled"

It feels a little prickly middle age
Like I'm so disconnected as a corroded unlit fuse
Still spitting brilliantly but dazed momentarily
Who is this man unjoined on a sun lit hill
He whose life hangs on by all these fringes

What is he suppose to do at this nadir with so few options being
    opened meaning nothing
When he's confused without much human placement
Resembling a protectant cover or cove
All temperament to plagiarize
One's short comings on brief road trips
I found in you some playful energy to enliven
Even when you spoke Elizabeth, Emily cleansing the soul
You sprinkled your aura into me, but what was the clause catching
    every pratfall on this 10th day of the year (2010)
Before Mayan theories become remedial and axes shift violently

Money pools also moved gallantly at Turf Paradise
And then the usual furor
Like the discord of swallow or geese
On a bestial path
There real lease to be our inhabitants as hidden herbs are God's
    love

But then the healthy gavotte toward you
As if I was walking blarney toward a yacht named "Street Cry"
    (honk) -07
Favoring the smothered air like smelts
You pulled a laminated note from your insole
With a point about me being cardinal forever and more than a
    remnant

I looked up at a smarmy sky, orchid and blue
With a dazed look of contentment between your crooked smile
    with
One felt nudge Sara soothed all panic before dawn at Troopers
Aren't these waiters, bartenders just cubs of comfort to the mind
When the Inn's are closed at 1:25 they still remain luminous to
    undefined
Infinity only Dylan could grasp in a ballad thinnest of instruments
With a clash and soft clamor of brilliance dazzles a few

"Instruction"

We all are pointless fodder
Just sons of bitches, little thrush
Commanded by the behemoth
Obscure as any day laborers without control on love of
community
Who prefer a helix of moral ground
But which like hedonism more than nature's hypnotic stare
Is a lion in a comforting place draping his power
Before marching like a gendarme unto heinous endeavors
The bow of manhood breaks, shrieks and then silence to an
insidious world
Loss is the voice that transcends time without liberalism or
instruction

"Magnetism"

He had this magnetic force you couldn't pass up when he walked
    into a room
Candle wick stood still as girls eyes adored him
As if he were a spoon or an actor in a continuous plot
Who hides them in a belfry for fun because their thin

He could work the Idyatt or any comfort dive
By noon or a calm afternoon or night
With a coolness of Noxzema or mountain's stinging air
Women would succumb to before a moon's surrender
To just shadows of light tapering

His mind sketched every one
On carbon bond paper with a sharp charcoal pencil – no. 2
The one with the arched eye brows was Ava Wexler
With a vague new you see in every window's charm
Is just that empty space of skepticism
Like the sureness of tomorrow

Before I took her hand
She knew I made plans
Whatever it was she liked in me
A boiling, rumbling joy and a rush of magnetism

"Lollapalooza girl"

It happened so presto squeezed like a logjam
At midstream pinching every passage except for fishes
You say nothing yet
Does that mean I'm at the helm of indifference
You were taught in Sunday school

What is it from you I must pilfer
If I'm not prejudice myrmidon even to your ranginess I admire
At 5'-6" by change
Fulfilling the ratio giving all man a choice between this
    psychodrama even unfolds
You were all sold to every landlubber now who becomes shunt to
    American roulette

"Lowering egos"

If you don't believe we are born entirely out of suffering
Than how can we love or die with dignity
Our breaths would be in haste

But somehow even children understand our world it seems
Someone give them a mint -57- Indian nickel to cherish
For having that undefined logic seldom seen in man today

But try to lower our egos share in the nourishment of things
Closest to nature an maintains that look at us with dark wings
Watching mankind collide

And still we elude to ourselves singularly
If just once we'd try to do without too much convenience
But not favors from the image of heat cultures
Rewired in straws of plenitudes beings bear something
Even if it's herbs grown in a garden to be tossed in semolina
And please help the seniors

The new bourgeons hides from the myth of corporate power so
    seedy and sine cure
New beats' selling incense or poppy seed
And brandishing laminated books of poetry with maps of interest
    inside
That read "nature's lost terrains in America, our hidden landscapes
You may be living close to a former underground railroad near
    Phoenixville

It doesn't hurt to be taken aback even by the Madoff scheme
Every user gains a reprise even from hog nosed mobsters
Because no one suffers alone
Recharging batteries during a cold Manitoba night
The Michelob bottles looked so staid in the garage dabbing and
Brushing them to our lips calming our innards as Gina Lynn
    stares from a poster

"Alien"

Staring at the lean gristle incensed in a pan
Move at midday wondering where it all went wrong
Associated to being novitiate at forty-three still alien
Later in that doorway, standing, staring
I only wanted you beside me awhile honey
As you pulled your hair out of that bunched net

Morph, quiet, but as weird as strange jazz sounds someone's
    motif
And when I reached the Inn's black macadam
It felt as if it was waiting to swallow me up whole
But I wasn't on the lam I was trying to free the incarcerate truth
But then you sprung from the boards without a word the world
    unfolds
When it all seems alien

"Subscribe" to –(passiveness)

Even great quarterback's wait passively on sidelines when their team losses ball control. Being passive is the buffer to timing and change. I'm sure it has a relation to Buddhism which we benefit from if not in a time of pain, but peaceful longing.

If I ever feel too submissive to the world or others I can become cleansed by the ginger of nature. Many might agree to never try to mollify passiveness because it is a strength greater than any vain glory and obscure as the beauty of vagrancy. All this in a subliminal way. I can't find much wrong in being passive it's how we utilize the sun in many ways even in making tea.

The only fear in being passive is becoming yeasty hoping we don't make a shutter step similar to equines. In the last serial portrait of living my mind became entranced to the servitude of a young lover or friend. It's all I ever wanted in a final passage before death's smile becomes you. Acknowledge the receipts, the will, build the parterre.

I have choose to think of passives someone I know or myself and their split screen meanings, comfort or not in knowing she's one too. Were often thought of being endeared from a distance. A good common trait of being passive is having the patience of a beaten down moth, the one's hanging on garage walls bogged by humidity.

Maybe we are the beautiful flitting last angels careless to respond to much of anything privy to their own conservation. We may love feeling contemptible at times. We all being in our own macrocosm not the typical masochists male or female.

I've wondered if being passive is all but a cured act before becoming the aggressor Coup-led as we are the patience of being passive up to a point. With this personality we do live below our means (some) of us, but can't the hand me down life be a cusp of certain denials.

To the ones who haven't made one aggressive call is that hour you show passion. Make use of everything around you all this nothingness. All our passiveness is it just a hind defense before spontaneously moving on. Maybe passiveness our greatest gift. It definitely culls us from temptation time and again. Passiveness should be as heralded as the arts or ancient trees along any savannah that saved a guile union soldier.

Passiveness wears a heady crown it keeps me from you doyenne, where my monsters' hide inside me begging for an upstart is also how you cumbersomely address me with curtness I never needed – or too much truth.

And these words I ail like nails to a coffin asserting to an independence not well deserved, is it. That started and labored, "ooh, ooh, ooh", as if your a resisting ohm. All that to a hobbled placement one needs no identity. Mine to another now, tomorrow maybe so (you) show me the passive quality that works completely. Sometimes it's a show of failure or just a different kind of twain retreat to the river or meadow.

And the stream poems a reminder I hope of lapping waves you can't wipe away.

"Brother (man)"

You may become the last vestige of my immediate family
That alone sounds so serious
Brother
Only yesterday we were coupled on grass fields for Town Toy
near Firestone, sunrise lane
with dirt for a mound where a pitcher stopped on a thin piece
of rubber
Stout tumid to knock us down but I made contact once on an
infield fly
Over the 1st-baseman's head and got on base finally without
shaking
Able to breathe thru a sky of blue or a few clouds dizzying our head
What happened to us, do we need the patch work of counseling
You got married long-after me at   first it seems like a
long-fly-ball
Outta-here salute (Valas)
You became so immersed in making it right, what's right now to
be encumber
You sound too desperate during our brief moments conversing as
if your me car-managed
Don't forget to tell her off for once, brother
It'll feel like you have vertigo at first
But when she begins to fully respect you again
She'll come back like any ebb
I hope you'll come to understand with mettle
Sooner than I did later life becomes a dribble not a timid maravich
drop for (3)
Despite what choices we make sacrifices similar to those glorious
lambs nothing really matters as Michael professed except your
own idealism and those three or four marks of existence
Ending selves of complete emptiness

"Climb"

Everyday it seems worst than the last with each climb
It's hard to see past the refuge and the scars lost steps in memory
And if the sun blasts thru for a day what then, feathers blow
   upward
From a nest freed from clay

Would I even hear your resounding voice filled with the usual
   mystic charm
For a 2nd-showing me what's obyetd art just an inception
Boy, reincarnate I've been ostracized too long that I can't
   remember
Yellow rayed flowers or Jen's croppy hair in that place of hollow
   opulence

You don't have to be a darting sunfish in the shallow mirrored
   waters
Seemingly refilled when glared upon
Before I find a reason for every rejuvenescence refreshed in this
   glass
And then you stood askance objectively behind on oasis and it's
   obstruction
Naked waving your hands like spring wheels from their onis

As if nothing was subsequent until a night surrenders to dreams
I'll never know if it was forged by a disembodied soul
I had during an hallucination my mind haltered back to reality
   slowly
Just a Prada handbag with scales of sequins with Dahlia imprinted
   in it's corner.

"Realness"

I felt so bogged down by surroundings and it's realness
that I alone could only blend or bequeath in handwritten words
tomorrow's clause like Flood in free agency castings and the
    spoilt

No longer can you denounce my mores
Some genuine even in my fiction life
You had become someone to me unclouded
Stars do reach out as I have from time to time
As I approach the indignities of aging
Somewhat ramble and fidgety

I wanted to tell you –
How you looked fetching on CTO's parking lot
A contour in balancing rarely imitable
Stretching my mind's time and immunity
As if I were continentally adrift
Until you quizzed me before contiguity and lavish drinks
Was just knowing you at all
And I wouldn't take back each contretemps ever

And if you ever came out of your coop
To prove this wasn't all fiction of hip-hop or passing vignettes
Against earth's grains or dirt
Where we danced on the edge of the Allegheny

"Blowing"

Fingers cranked to a cool, calm blow on a cigarette
While you held a loopy grin
For a second the way a sow does
And then you hopped between limestone and weeds in a
    quagmire
Dangled loosely
The sun was like a spangle on your clothes of silk
From China or India
You were embarked to the back seat of a car
Making each specification known
In her own quiet language before a roam colored sky
She kept her leather sandals on
As she oohed it sorta seemed refractory
With a rush of musk in the air almost onion like
Your olive eyes sublte to my old world values
Derobing everythying about me

First I laid close to your secretiveness
Holding back time
As the moon's lens captures and becomes a lost capsule
Waned to truth

"The contortionist"

Look at the contortionist
Never a fiction acrobat to children wriggling like a pretzel
He doesn't know himself, they or whom
But he makes up their capsule world

He just knocks everything in his sights
Living, tried, conformed or true
As if he woke up from a sky of blue
Alongside Sal paradise and those Seasame St. characters

"Scrambling"

Nearing all the ending bending curves
So purposeful never glad
My mind now scrambled like eggs hardened in a cardboard box
No, I don't believe in cracker jack dreams
Now, I forgot all these errands all that I had to do
Do you know that feeling as if someone's scraping your insides
But then I touched that pocket of muscle behind your knee
Warming every finger
And I was even more thirsty on a Thursday thinking of that
     dancer
Joanna Krupa from ""DWTS"
Showing a magazine featuring, honoring gluts like morsels
As my fingers scrambled to the next page to a girl named Kim

"Opened without answers"

You slipped through my hands like wrong formed wrought
Bared against cold wind
Nothing I could do about your regular, ductile wanderlust
And whoever you casually sought
To beat me to my knees, but I cannot beg

And the only love I see is in tall grass with rollicking butterflies
Steady as a ridge hung on fine cloth
Love for some men so genuine and quite slum
You layed dusty as a worm moth
And all you could say as if your voice was in repose,
"I use to date him."

How trusting fate is sometimes when were nearing our end
Is that beauty will drag you down always
With it only a guarantee dwindled as a Buddhist soul retreating
Remember love is twisted and knurled
Like the wrought iron that aging hands cling too

"Beckon"

Fat chance to make something happen
Before being hangdog on secure hemp
I might be in harmony with a stranger
That harbors and holds back my decline with every stout
     memento
Born on continuation one's I haven't dreamed of yet

Slim chance to make a reserved waitress mine
Her Goth skin and dark hair fastened like a taut Oreo
I couldn't like any less – you beckon
Stooped down like an enveloping flower petal dangled
To pick up my Belmont umbrella and then we left
Before I became anymore dumbfounded and restless as leaves
     strewn

I humbly held you close
Shellacked from the rain at 5th- and cherry
As you breath held close on a brisk night like smoke
Your eyes looked bereft of something

As yellow gum drop lights carom from a police cruiser
Shimmer on your clothes benignly as you whisked me to more
     splendor
And these exemplar heated car seats
Warm as a summer's white cap
The only thing that comes between
In the sound of swishing traffic with slow vigor and those
     unnormal stars
I nicked because of you
Not one ever beguiled they just confuse destiny

"I and you"

I and you
Stranger than nature's fixtures and the big bang's initial deprivation
Learning no subtle messages except this great openness
The elocution of the speeding wind on that hickory tree's leaves
Reminds me of those races and you
Or he who went the fastest a substructure to even a president
Or a general whose mercurial rise didn't last

And, am I just a passing soul who got nothing too substantial on
	the side of humans treated like an unsubsiding meth high
Or an ecclesiastical viper alone with me on a mesa
More tender is the ice claw on your milk bottles I bring to your
	door –
Steeped in snow mowing like a merry go round and in a stilted
	language
You said, "Hello, come inside I'll take care of the stipend over a
	crisp fire crackling like pressed lips
I and you pleasantly tapping each planned vagary
An inclination to capably bend you
And from where I sit fixated to your charm
You never seemed tawdry as most waitresses wearing those
	baubles
And with a little A-do or refrain
Except you rooting smile or wiggled purple painted toes
We become round about and rove to infinity

"Rolling on to one"

As the rain taps, slides down, drums below my roof
And cracked chimney mercilessly
Usually when were betrothed in a still sadness one finds fishing
with a light wind that awakens us it is nature's call that
summons us
Carefully and abruptly to take some aim or direct others

Why take it for granted now would you destroy all that you can
afford for Allah
Or see you forever
At the end of the day
It's rich plains the sun rolls over onto
When it is the only rescue after being let down constantly, isn't
it

So mankind don't try to control the weather
It gets madder than all could ever be, it champions on like Ray
Lewis and Manning
Pray your protected from it's mad rush
An occasion it's like cloved to many hooves
And then it changes abruptly like bi polar people who ask
something abound
About Brett returning to Mississippi and these buddies of yore

"Bound by nature"

Massive rows of sinewy old hickory
As if they were heavily armed soldiers guarding fortresses
Assured monuments of natures enclaves
Where you surrounded me to you I never quite knew
As the country lake stared at us with a slick grin

You whisked me with your hand to walk under that old 160'
    long truss
Between two canceled low-banks like tubs
We rolled around nimbly before night blindness
And then, we nestled under those man-made beams
And strewn burlap against a cushiony ground so coffee like

As I closed my eyes and touched your mound
Just to forget a dilapidated now truncated world begging for
    stimulation
At a time I became impervious as those marked trees
These trusting bees deliver nectar as colored specks nature's
    postmen

"The Gnomes Gate"

Under the rich soil the gnomes wait
Near the black wrought metal gate for their collection plate
Of tin foil and nickels
Glazing the metal bars with spittle
One whispered, "Tomorrow we'll steal that guys antique spittoon
   with the fancy carvings."
So droll these sport figures with names like Tommy John
Batters waiting at a white rubber plate on a pitched ball whistling
   thru the air the way aliens have evaded us
While the air changed to a smell of genuine before a catstrophe
Only gnomes could endure it's captivating belch of horrors lay
   doom.

"Track down"

In the mental illness of my mind still flashes of brilliance
While a heart flutters like a wing-less bird, mine to have gargoyles
    watch over us with frowns
Refuged from the past is tomorrow so close to being road kill
As everyone's let me down cyanide drains the last restraints out
    of living
Some use antifreeze

If in pretense it dawned on me in our new millennium
What all this routine is called
Bad luck is everyone's first person prose so gutsy to exceed
Bad luck pressed you to your soul so you could lastly think of
    nothing
As real or good or bad and be calm

While writing these feelings down
Because nothing is steady in decorum not even one call from
    you
To be available no matter what chore your doing
I botched your independence borne on eccentricity and pulled
    out the twisted arrows
From our own arrogance we break and darner
Floated like balloons over rivers that Corrad would never eschew

Such gallant fuss inexorable to us while infiltrating
To encompass your soul and body
Haven't you found yet who's extrasensory
Or am I just the faint trace of your perception was waning

The precursor to what remains
No habitable existence as I exculpate every dream I had
And banquet on the youthful to find something useful
To the touch Lisa's clenched purple sweater skirt
Bashing in a dead day's glow as she were a gem
And all she said was "I'll tell her, I will."

"This labyrinth"

Driving thru the dark bridle of North Coventry
The calm minds restitution of revolutionaries and their
   labyrinth
While the street lights steadily shine
As ribbed sheets ghostly encumber the waters
On the Schuyllkill
Fidget as if their an embodiment of what's real

Strained like my purpose of fitting built on hard work
And a contained fiber striated with colors
Onward the slow drive and whistled tires such as in sea shells
Tired as my schlep body and feet;
Nature as regular as my screwball self, reliable as an almanac
   decrees our faith
I wait in winter for its decimal change will wake me
As all the minds passages narrow in time to Lou's small town

"In hiding"

Stood at this pole
Chances thin as Lindsay's thighs
Wanted nothing
My particulars elusive and different from most
Never was one with the careful boast
Even at a street corner nature vents for our attention

The way I do at the bar's divide
Bartenders talk with fragmented joy
This cost of deviates where of coincidently
Worlds collide some in retrograde
And I'm passing thru to my indifference
And every indignity to you solid in my stoic mind
Felt like a cook who wallops steak before sprinkling a crafty
    marinade

Come on, spark my disillusionment
These crossroads must bare something prolific
Even if it's only a smile
I might only be here a while to stroke passion

These indignities like small tree reminders
The boy lost on trails without a compass before dusks' gauntlet
Relays a message to all wildlife even snails

I can't even find one whose as charismatic and splendid as I am
I keep looking, but she never comes back and nothing even
    close-Ian
A portrait of my soul in hiding without a claim
We could be a clever combinement, you know – now hurry

Before I'm whittled down to drawn bitters and the last straw
What an arrangement you make a perfect table
Hands knuckled to carpet on your knees, elbows inward in
    anticipation
When the light goes down
All you have is the veridical moon supple unto day break
And I who supplant all feeling staring at those purple painted
    pistils
On each toe and at the guilt where I hid your keys so you wouldn't
    leave too soon
If just to hark the sounds of a 19th century home lapped in your
    arms
As the grand-father clocks hand twist in decorum
Two calm witted ghosts whisper in their own code in hiding clues
    to our yawning dog

I like myself some
Why don't you like me enough as (two) parts of something
You get a free passport with me – babe
To room against my pliant nature
Lock these doors the way you want to be screwed
Bring it on lithe and lusty one
A beggar's banquet of sorts, flowers so pristine they strangle
    thought bring it to the table, talk, then eat
Leave the state of your vice
Never waver from caprice just whisper
The way wind swishes velvety curtains

"Connection"

Between these old Victorian braced walls
Is a circle without closure
Where a circuit board of vague thoughts lay
Where an artist can write about someone's proclivity
Versus longing to just wilderness
And there is no call to closure

But a connective one, each word a timed beat of the heart
How is it that I can provoke one, you
When your not around anymore
Physically in my presence to wile away all that hidden charm
Connected to the unordinary types called us of course
Both eccentric to living below their means
And you said, "at least you take the time to feel."
Is that so terrible, sometimes it is

Where I sit like a poised monk treading time
Similar to marines splashing upon water in control
Can you sense a burst of energy
Connection linear as a sun or cupped moon
As I watch over you minding that your safe

What is it I'm most attentive to? If everything
Connection soft was fingers squeezing a new Rawlings ball with
    bravado
Why we didn't get past the first pitch, is anyone's guess humanly
    possible?

Connection
How do you easily forget me, I could push harder, to ? – Twain
And I don't mean to be harmful
Pressed against Houdini's watered chest riddled in chains, whited
out
Connection, free me, peer back
Life is assaulting me, now, tomorrow
Connection, we need no plan
Just borrow my spirit before we get old
Is only a phrase for those with no assistants

"Against celestial bodies"

You rushed to me, timidly said, "Ahh where do you want to go."
As time reigns its mark on a stark night
A bard's words mark you, you matter some
We tried to suspend it, time by being tickled
As if we were characters in surrealism not ever divisible, watching
    a documentary
But our time as thin as sparrows plucking food
Cherishing it as a mind's supplement, sublimely you kneeled on
    the floor
The heel of your sneaker pressed, knobbed against my groin
As you showed me your artifacts, mine also close to marquetry
We could've freed each other for servitude
But all I'm feeling is the lack
Pruned from real happiness between these squared corners
Curved to wilderness dull as a dolman
I think, "are the suns more mightily than God's swords."

"In a famish land" – (Stands courage)

1 blockhead blossoms alte in life
Blessed just enough (by) God's strength an inheritance
To float above mainstream
Didn't last past the blitz that began in 07, the new great divide
These shining pricks glistening in full stride

The (NWO) ideology
A sweeping swath made us faux pas created mayhem
You got your greasy bailout and steak typically dada
The fun employment cot fava beans not fetching anytime soon
Like Goyim were the pulled sweater of damned sheep
And you got cashmere from Malaysia

I will not buckle to your plan or cycle
All life now a spoilt dandelion
Each of us split like a live wire to a dangled incorrigible fuse
Found a scrupulous lawyer to me on disability
So I wouldn't lose

Took a page from your principles before more famish
I could no longer be the lull in your deception
And what's next and forthcoming valor
Alen's Patriots with a forte to squeeze back every prick's dream
    of elitists

I saw on a pre-teens shining Schwinn a bulky sticker in red, white
    and blue that
Said, "Speed the new age minutemen to take back democracy,
Socialism is politically corrupt it must die, save the commoner."
    Assemble.

"Root and "Route and rootless"

You gave it all,
Until you couldn't anymore soldier on
You know someone who did the same many times
But still some don't get it, never will each bold sacrifice
Mom said you fell hard on ice laminating yourself between it and
     snow
Her stifling voice said your getting old, you look so bad
And what is so sad, don't want to go down
The same strewn path what's life without living the experience
I don't want to falter in mid-life
Go down the same immobile stretch
I'll find my own strange way, Dad mystic as Van Gogh
Your advice that caustic burning wit was embarrassing a bit
Because you made me better

"Soft Bears and Wolves"

The snow boulders stood solemn
From the last wintry storm
Looked like still frozen polar bears
Weary from their habitat
Waiting as us for the next non easter
On a Wednesday they should've named 13
Hours earlier employees in restaurants cashed out early
The storm playfully lashed us batted on eye lid
Until curling inward by midday
Fir trees outside wearing thick armed sleeves
Over green army uniforms covered by increasing white powder
With ease the Montg. County bus to the geriatric center,
Passed the snow route fork beside my house
Inside grade school brats exempt from being constructive
Watched Thomas and Friend about talking trains narrated by
    Carlin
In the frying pan there is no fat
The snow outside even plied to emanate domain
Reminds me of a world completely in respite and lost
And things I don't like tossed in salads that are green –
The eyes of Tanya I love with a tinge of chestnut color
Tomorrow, early morning restitution,
Shoveling against wind and nature
In a trap preserved for the richly wolves
Pressed against you salt water lips
I stayed sangfroid thru a coursed day
I'm not sure of anything or how that young thing- Sara
Lays her head in contentment
Charitable to this unbearable world even if wrongly censured

"Weighing"

Placating tellers
Tara and Trish searching to their imago
Waiting on oft opened Tom and especially Tim
One embodies me in private
Tara's charm like a soothing opiate that weighs heavily
Trish subtly the same as if they tinkle all my immunity
Without a whim didn't get much further without a brazen
    word-
Now I still see their vision across these counters
Where flyers about investments lay
But they've gone to other jobs as if to subterfuge us
Without telling their story but hearing the gist of mine
Must all life be hinged by the subterranean encampment of ties
When I needed your quirkiness, you said, "I can be indecisive."
And also is there anything else I can do, "of course you may."
As I'm bowing to acceptance gradually to any immediacy

"Before more waning"

If true love wanes
And is something external alone, surely tenuous
Then why do all my good intentions of you
Never lessen in time

From where I sit my mind is constantly dangled loose
But I'm not Houdini either
It's as if I was hanging on to sharp edged crags
To always feel even on urge can be a constant hindrance
I could end up the taint at the end of the deep blue
Because we went on a tangent without enhancement

Do you feel as if you'd been lagging behind
The way of westward settlers of yore
And now not yet a meeting for a tete-a-tete of dim thought
For once I'd surely tell you what you need
Before you see
Part my insufferable pain, are we just an interim plan

"Standing at a threshold" – (thinking of you)

I was thinkin of you, and what I believe, sadly
Driving along polished dry salted roads the sun used as a
    softener
Wondering stealthily if you had a valentine
Thou, it's none of my business;
I wanted you to know I was thinking of you
As forgotten as any hero or sideline player
To most everyone one sunflower needing redemption
And I don't mean to super-impose but I do
Without needing a parenthesis of sorts or being genuflect
You know the superlative meaning of 4-lettered sprinkled words

"Respectable"

Gather something she can't mull as subsidiary
So she'll have something to say respectable
Isn't the moment a timed call to urge or curb manner
And then we find out everyone's bid about something
Isn't it absurd when your graying but a youth at heart
What you told me wasn't in deferment about another
Whilst the flowers of romance danced like a wolf in our heads
And I could see all the treachery in this trembling world
So I believed in trees I watch in a pacific morning
Because they couldn't tell me they were hurting
Even when their neutral colored chips lay strewn at their roots
But their not pearls shining in the sand that hypnotize
To lessen our memory or train of thought
The way customers like stretching tendril do
And I have nothing to go back to except dull transition

"Paring – (to goodness)"

It may be commonplace to think the comely sea
With it's immense size
Just jeer seemingly at catastrophic east coast blizzards
Not the calming drink from Dairy Queen

I don't know who hemmed (stitched) this paranormal weather
    pattern
In other ways I was already straddled
Now I must waddle like a puppy through the white snow
A colossus of cluster
That giant bear claw you salivated for at 9 am
No not the iced donut, soda jerk

The storms like you
It needs to straddle and berate it's elders
Who still find enlightenment of every kind
What a choice word meaning I would need a behaviorist
One can free this madness to make you equable

I may as well settle for watching fierce equestrians and Savannah
Or sip the occasional expresso listening to seniors
Maybe I'll join the Cambridge Apostles
They seem a society of decency rarely found

Oh, what storms and cultists do
When I heard you laugh
It's sound appears like a distant cry of a flat footed tortoise
Lapsed from crushing leaves where goop lay

I use to bath in your las civiousness
Now it's just a lawless twisted memory
One so entrenched hidden without any dispensation
Fated to mythology and the polarization of bears
Never in transgression
It's easier to postulate the late greats out of Michigan
Too numerous to mention, but poised Trammel
Soft as Jack's promo down the hall resonates it's magic

"Lesson to be found"

I think we should find
Other ingenious outlets
Even if it is nature's plot
To be an artist with props that fill
I can almost hear the beat of the wild

While our intake to each is mal-nutrition and lacking
I feel as I'm the inmate who left the ranch
And came back fluttery
To a macerated drying inlet
That once nourished itself by rain
With little equability left
I found enrapture
And a key the sun made fluorescent

"Station to station" – (in plengency)

Rambling along like zimmy
Every departure predominant as before another urgency
Any falsehood would say he's rogue
As the way the media depicts politics so ratings soar

Maybe he's just running from the world
Being reticent and looking at nature's blessing
Now, the station stop at Missouri
Receptive to watching aristocrat women with petals/feathers in
    their hats and warning like peacocks
And retrograde strangers
Before going down another slated track

The air was crisp
Landing me as Montgomery Alabama
Ending a dream where people did the beguine
Where I met you
Dressed coyly in soft suede

My mind became suckle before I left the platform
Birds waved their wings and then descended
You rubbed your fingertips against my engraved buckle
Looked up and gave a suitable smile so cry

As the passengers filed along the east side
I gave one two twenties, winked and said,
"Don't tell em Bob was here." As if I was the poster boy
For the most wanted.
And then I asked her if she wanted to room some like Kerouac
To undisclosed locations from station to station
Between the yonder engrossed by nature and you, you, you

"involving"

The last film of my being was shredded and slowly a place of
ruin.

I don't know where I've been for fifteen years, the orbs of my life
here and there.

One stared to the unseen laid gunpowder on a bar table as you
and I scurried through a doorway

You could've weaned me to be happy for awhile instead we passed
each other and left few to this day ever to be enchanter

It just seems I'm so bereft of everything and so crazed with a
berth nothing cognate

Nobody comes along among the banter until I became lastly
brogan

You could see through me to something good

You were the bract of all my growth internal when I was stumbling
and rakish

Just your scent made me gasp for pleasure

Seated against plush carmine leather

A rangy and speckled spider crept fantastically low between each
star's glaze

Listen you can hear breathing distinctly the hark of an angel

Sipping in skin pretending to be blowsy, but your just like the
left who ascends all

"The doubled bifold that stares blankly"

Some people think they have exclusive gloom
That's how models appear to me in cigarette ads
Others think the darkest days only belong to them
What's a patriot to do
In Haiti liken to New Orleans but worse no relating tame just
    doom
Reminds me of you and I doubled to painful thoughts
That black bifold stares back in vain, stitched to my pocket

Not double mint scented and glad
It's as if were that buoy flagged against a shoreline swishing along
    with time
What happened to a world where there was once fraternity
Now everyone takes sides left, right using rigmarole

Too much doubt, unproven messages after the greatest election
    turns to a debacle
If we let it
Everyone's dossier looking blank especially Presidents who set the
    (NWO) trap
A system preventing freedom or inventing jobs
And the banks won't loan only to bailouts now they just soldier
    on

The middle-class just doubled plowshared to ever increasing
doom
And tomorrow I just may lose more dopamine
Until you step in that door Sara
I just don't care anymore

Without healing glue to supporting life boats across two shores
Just what am I waiting for
Is it to see the face of doom
I don't think I can go without a fight
To romp home safely

"Behind us"

I had goose bumps when I heard he had died
As if he were family, but only an author who loved what he left
    behind
Words like granules to a percolator
A tongue would sip
All this reminds ourselves what we want the most
We cannot have
Lest it could destroy us

Something someone like M.G. makes a study of, our relationships
As those who fall between bell curved nonsense
Isn't even a thread of who we are
And being outside the middle with all the others

She hates it when I address alternate ways of living
I could never stay so shallow just to one
And all that's abound many still bear in likeness
To me

And that wasn't exacting change; but the truth
And one time a dark haired beauty/stylist tied a tag
Around our wrists
For someone
Unknown having a birthday party at Canal St.
Even new age
Reveling in with stranger
Before they go back to the nether
What's left behind us
Has no finality
It could be like sorting gems

"Inside finding"

Any Buddha enthusiast would say
Don't look outside
To a grieving world of
Rape, murder, lies and deceit
You will find all that's uncouth and worthless junk

But inside ourselves a rebellion's wish to start something fresh
Without beggars or hanger-ons
When we meet it'll be when
I move past tranquility and peace
Your tilting apparition like curling smoke
Coming across white light

Between the shadows and the mirrors
Like a La Chapelle
Glanced hazy photos of humbled sights and figures
Still and dancing in our brains

Vaguely noticeable hiding in their purity
Still I look to find myself (Nikki's) complex
Prepared to nurture, delve, prosper, or falter
Buying a waitress's look airy as in May

What did I expect past your lemon scent under my nails
Some sort of infinity

"Sharing greatness"

If failure is the common axiom
I could see it in the face of family oddly enough
Then why can't we escape it,
I wonder if Socrates knows the answer
Or is it exclusive to only one
Be not afraid, try, try again
He may say we can't be great at all things
Even rudimentary things such as zippers
Hide leave open crossing school yards in winter
It would be great to find one commoner
Who reads me or even laughs at all that perplexes
And if the flock didn't follow
You didn't fail completely
I remember Leach and Ruffin reviving careers in the American
    League as relievers
Yes, again, you didn't fail completely
Gradually someone will sit at a desk waiting for Starbucks
Slowly that hourglass life relieves us
But it's easier to make a dent for someone else
Than to feel at all like a demagogue

"Bearing solemnity"

When my expectations were stalled
Like waiting passengers at O'Hara
I was never felled by solemnity
It was eased by meditation
On forgotten ridges or

Between Victorian walls that hear nothing
Mankind was their source
Mine wasn't quite found in San Francisco or Birdsboro
I was never completely serious

So I somersault around importance, still do
Unless it's a book I'm reading purposely sedentary of course
Or a bet carefully made
To forget another's name, speeding to God willfully
The one and only I'm not solitary to
When I can't shave points to a bad ending
I know that with all that solemnity
I'll be sedulous tomorrow to something
Simply because he is soothingly there preparing

"Urged on"

When I felt so sorrowful about not moving on
Past these medial points Frost endured for others
Something happens so mellifluously
When I feel so low down ready to break
And then I become creative and write selflessly
Now who'd want to shed that demon as now I'm seemingly on
    automatic

"Balancing act"

Is there a balance
Between our temperament and nature
I tend to be calm peering past man made things while driving
Those fluorescent lights watching our vacant industrial
    buildings
Along industrial Blvd
Where you could hear the screech of metal once
Now most communication is from the telepathy nature brings
    us
It's message not to outdo or outlive us
I shouldn't have to drive to rural areas because of eminent
    domain
To just see hulking hickory with those brown beads at every
    base
Mankind stop disturbing mature even a teaspoonful
You saw what happened in Chile and Haiti
The unseen forces of nature can turn us to naught
Can you imagine dead bodies picked up by cranes or yellow
    bulldozers
Where limbs dangle loosely on thick silvery blades navigating to
    dump sites
When will the physical have a plan with nature that's a balancing
    act
I need it's crafty wonder world
Before aging leaves me with no mettle
Except to pull a shaking cup of cocoa to my lips

"Intervene"

London adorns his toys with a fascination glued
Like close-knit lovers
And then he taps my hand and says, "open"
Those Tupperware totes
Giving us a break, I hear him say, "Choo, choo."
He know it's okay to live remote away from the discipline of the
    city

An occasional train whistles down across Rice St. and High
Still keeping me uninterested by repetitive sound
When I'm trying to sleep
But not the thong perched on the dresser dark as night
It's sequin's reflect a moon's light
You intertwined your fingers with mine
As I lay sentient wishing I was young and ungoverned again

"Leaking" (to)

Love is my dear just a fire
Waiting to be doused
Because there is only one infinite
You didn't know you had it in your containment
You felt it's fire you shrewdly abandoned with a casual shriek
Over a phone voice dismantles it's empowerment
But what about this time alone
Leaks nothing with losers you don't adore – for Jewel's losses

"Enlighten"

Some with BFA's say start a story with a list:
Eve is sensual
Eve is like a rainbow so tranquil
Eve is all that's wickedly in the word fulfillment
Eve's eyes could break a man's will
Eve also eyes all junkmen handily as the ride
Eve is now gone but hem lined to my mind somewhere
All those hugs and kisses
I miss you half-point
And I still haven't found an equal to go with godliness
Just goose bumps that bad apple and leave you shivery

"Slowly"

The day lingers on as leaves remain so crisp and still because it's
    not summer yet, still 42
But it is only 1:0 am the time people, dogs sleep
To awaken to defining moments slowly
One's that don't perpetuate to grace
And when did making money cause the masses social gain
As most everything is pretense the same as before unless your
    oddly different
Each day lingers on trust much of anything except a bird's
    search
Unless your celebrity is the focus; just how pained is Lindsay
I'd love to meet her sober for two months.
For I to have treaded on like a new swimmer
Paddling on tiresomely to the end somehow near
If I could just hear a soft voice say… then I'd know time didn't
    trick me,
Was I what you liked and craved
I bet, I bet your life

"At midnight

The way the young crowd at midnight look at you
To see the undefined aura
Before ransacked aging
I felt for the startled robins
Idling as a car but tied to a bar's perimeter
As Charlotte waited for her sister to take a break
From playing with a guy unplugged so did I – in turn
As she said to astonish for goodness sake
Give her the note from his silvery gum wrapper
And then I did cleverly the next day

Before she went away on vacation I was approached first
Because I gave her a book about Hunter
Later I thought of her in that pitched tent
Being the fevered stuffing in her panties
I can't believe how the mind vents every hallucinogenic truth
As I settle for the scent of a fresh picked rose
Deters all temptation is it badder than dying

"Until now"

I never thought; until now
I'd be as lonely as tools or supplies in a shed hanging on
Even the sly evidence of mice left abruptly
They couldn't find the bird feed
And one got lost in a pool that swallows

How defiant the lonely to find a beat's way
Short on a path that will beat you
In any way that's humanly possible

"I could leave"

I could leave you all because of the insults
That lead to more humiliation
Over 15 years of salt on open wounds
That need's a soothsayers spoon fed remedy

I don't need any of you any longer; I've had enough of your
    punctuation
Just the call of the wild wind delivering my soul
And the plate you made
To a kindness with hints made by the sound of languished
    owles
Plus the kind found in water sheds or a San Diego sunset
Drifting against the vagrant backdrop of the world

Someday you will know how it feels to be crushed by everything
    living repeatedly
And unconditional was someone else's dream or God's indulgence
    never crude
To feel your hardened hear tof stone
Doubtful it could cross over me

Because in death there is no finality
It washes away all hurt for some and every insult minor or
    forgotten
Will leave you to your tears and vices
Someday the someway my mind was thrashing against
    plowshares
When I was called an idiot

"Adventuring"

Twain's real name
Similar to my own but missing the T
My initials the same as Tom Clifton the prudent jockey
No wonder i was on aloof adventurer in my borrowed teens
Never rushing to any judgment either;
Is that why I liked one black girl with a frilly fro

I took the wisdom from two grandmothers
One whose eccentricity I finally bought
And the other who could speak eloquently as her father
Even about a roadside bar's Tom Collins

Is that why my father was in the Jaycees
And I still don't know what that meant,
Did it relate to theology or a cult of misinformation
As I fought against time to be with nature
Before darkness arrived

We climbed high hills above obscure bridges
Where vacated railways stood rusted against strewn grass
With thin railing to save you from the Schuykill river
Where Bob swung from until I turned my head ghostly
Who knew one day we'd be fighting on either side of extremes
To find a centrist like Palin is better
Then any Hollywood liberal, and I am for the arts
Remember Red Skeleton and Art Carney
Not to overlook the importance of adventure

Dad am I dulling this perky prose
Because you left out all the insight of spelunking
Alongn the river beds of York plenty of unmistaken yore

"What was I"

You rounded others' worlds
While I was broken
A heal to your deception with Splayed spokes
And you never told me anything
Why you left me and what was i
Due to circumstances long ago
I now might find amusing

All you lovers buried in crimson sand
I've grown from abusing pain
While you crested but still remain pensive to this day
I remained true to nothing but words

And how could you just say, "I use to know him."
What a clause to know women really aren't affected by men
As if I were a non entity
Without an epitaph that's worthy – for Joan

"Ourselves to depend on" (Know)

They depend on us –
The little ones just to survive upon arrival
All tidy in strict regiments of play
But take something away from them like Windex
Oh, how screechingly London bellows
I felt the same privation constantly
Aren't you lucky I don't walk away
If I did you'd never escape my mind

Pain like this rain on my cheeks now sallow
15 years later you wiped tears off my casket
With a white Asian silk scarf I bought you at Bloomingdale's
You may not like hearing this – Narissa
But, take care of them." For they depend on us,
Don't throw them off the wharf
Just because I loosely sinned
When I was out of helter mostly
Like a messed washing cycle
Spurting at different intervals to be mediocre
When bad missions failed something was saved
Every sacrifice prevented further damage unto ourselves
Remember the voices of the dead like something Kennedy said
    about doing unto others
Suspended in time like Ivory Snow bubbles
And that girl on the detergent box

"Stifling plight"

I sometimes hear bells toll
When I walk by back to my house
From our cracked sidewalk
It's as if they want me to hear them
Their purpose to arouse my curiosity
And come into this catholic church;
But I gave up on believing things
Except when I need God to prance

"Don't be afraid of hurting"

You could laught at my hurt
Hold it against me like a carved Incurved stone
Are you a she-devil and a (Leo)?
For the soul cannot shed, only eclipse
Ones who are simply caprice

I've been hurt and burned so much
But I can't hate the evil-doers
This hurt so puzzling and I still count
The ways past pain and frailty
Is the strength I find inside
Maybe because I went to Sunday school
Or just revel in the envy of being part Brother
And I can't , won't go back to the burrow
Of the once lived where shelter and
Passiveness collide

Happily for you I guess
To be alone, but I don't real know do i
Instead I haven't checked those quarters
So don't be afraid of hurting me
Companion of fortitude
Call instead you know your brooding
Just joking marigold

"Gravity so ingratiating"

I couldn't bring myself
Down these stairs because gravity is lawlessly corrective
Accustomed to writhing is for the lonely
Hanging jilted on a cliff
So I walked to this chair anyway
And thought how even a single rose
Couldn't belie cheerfulness
Until I write about nothing
Or her particulars from head to toe
Each one passed my mind between my eyes
Like silk silted patterns on ribbons or scarves
Writhing away
All this time spent spend thrift
Until you touched my hand better than falling to a smart strike
      to exact change
Against these prickly thorns uncouth razors
And then onto spark my deadliness
With one last flame so courageous
To lay curled next to a stranger
Who needs forgiveness

"Fanciful"

My house engulfed by sounds of unruly kids
But not by whelps needing all that fanciful wheedling
To lay in their stray beds
Dog's nestled to a cow's ear and straw
Until someone enters the front door
Wondering who's the inmate innkeeper
All sharing in God's inventiveness

Jaydon's esteemed child drawings at Christmas
Through to summers
And your sentient rigors of motherhood
Makes time inordinately impossible to bed you

"One time"

Once or twice
I fell between the lines of platonic love
A seldom seen realm of today
While onlookers smiled with contempt
But I never pulled close enough
To the saran rap of onion skin
And it's delight
To know or dab in your olive colors
So strikingly beautiful on that day

"Hounded by denial"

You are always an anchored
Like a bird in cast iron
With a paper mache for wings
Thick as the molding on heating pipes
Denying us both
Just when I wanted to take off
And share the world with others
I'm sorry that's a biblical right
Maybe one below the papal
As you stay tucked like a duck
On Lake Swanson being denied of everything
But Sara Lee cake
And wetted toes
The little heads ducked for croutons
Making a wave in delirium
As my picture in your pocket dusted the ground

"Disintegration of man"

Where did all the dismay lead?
We were the puppets in the reign of industrialists
If I find another puzzle piece that's tricked
Would I forget
I still have a life even if it's askance
And contorted as ballet dancers with integrity
Or would I crumble with the leaves stuffed in that rain gutter
So I followed your burgundy scent
And a hand that took me away to immortality
The kind that masks Keith's skull ring
Before the dynamics of the new age crumbled the simple man
And I know of rich men in the arts who don't even have a cell
    phone

"Insular"

I randomly see this Hispanic family
Walking on High street
A rakish man, his girl friend in white sweats
Pushing a coach effectually
And a mother following close behind them

Because of stereotypes I'm afraid to give them a ride
Are we Americans that insufficient and narrow?

I guess, two sides and a rankled GOP
Can't come to terms any days on health care
One can't dicker with capitalists
If not for the dichotomy
Were all the same

Ask that family or all the one's
Who don't believe in equality
If not for them you wouldn't be ensconced by wealth
Why must empathy only be shown in a clouded dream

"Demarcation"

Certain people's line of generation not showing much proclivity
Just likeness of eccentricity
Or accepting the slow descend from liquor
Like leafless aged trees potted downtown
But in time you shed all that's profound
Is Savoir faire
You set aside words of wisdom as though they were a creed
The things I've done to find affection
You couldn't give being clued
Wasn't because I'm with another

I don't really all pronouncing a need a kind of sinning
They do say blondeness comes from inherited health not dye
And how do I make my honor
Stand for something
When I'm just your disembodied soul

Remote as country moss growing on stone
Why can't you set me aside, the time I said, "what takes you so
    long."
As your wheels grazed along 422
Then came to a settling halt
Letting me be your hub was comforting
Like we kids huddled watching a DVD on the world's origin

"What happened"

Some people say what happened
Hemingway was fractured and pureed his brain
And what about Captain Lou
And our pusillanimous leaders
The bleeding heart evangelists building franchises
Is it better not to follow someone's lead
And me not following the sovereign dream
To build on what's plutonic and chaste

What did I do to make you leave
What was the special effect to make you come back
It's nice to know you can deal with all things
Pragmatic
Even when that hoof this the wire

"Just thinking"

Driving through God's country where nature is tender
I feel the weight of the world removed
The smell of hearth baked goods behind me
To my back I see an Eagles Jersey
In a beetle rigid Toyota
Kaitlyn didn't work today at Achenbach's
Or was finished
And I'm minding the road with vendors up ahead
Trying to sell barbeque chicken
And I'm just thinking of all that's behemoth up ahead
How do you say hello to the prettiest girl
Now that she's buried and dead
I still hear her say goodbye so grudgingly
And in some guise returns in naked thought
Like this place in God's country despite modernization he sees
    three
That not all capitalism is bad
Looking at Shady maple you give back guarantees

"Pacing floors"

In the narrow confides, love's crawl space where we reside
We can't reach ourselves much to know our deprivation
You are truer to the little ones pacing the floors constantly and
    clumsily
To the exactness of chores that can wait it's as if your looking for
    entrails
But there isn't even a living nearby

The slur bed vacillate our minds to be punctual but not in the country
Where we spin slowly I thought I was a pundit with a vision like
    Burroughs
But I keep coming back to the same place as you and pace the
    upstairs
When your sleeping
Because I want to feel my madness equally in every room before I
    feel it's pierce

I can't sail away on a punt anymore than you can change
But I went especially no where because of stubborn pride
And the steps I made a curb for insomnia or arthritis
Of all the over play dreams I haven't had burning a hole in tomorrow's
    desire
So you could harangue or laugh
And it's not a coincidence to feel every presentiment, I do
At these exact moments of precision while resting are to someone
    else
I just wrote to bear our common or bizarre differences
Is that someone else is like us

You may vaguely know or never met
Their tangible force
Is the tint of longing
With a tansy taste and jocund smile

"Awareness"

Did you or I ever think of
How little we need, but awareness, nourishment, maybe love
Now that's something we look at askance
Driving by Martinsville to see the loss of industry jobs for miles
Ghostly here to lost kingdoms without revitalization
You see in Phoenixville's vision

This unemployment really bolsters levied friendships
Two guys confer in a bar
About not having a plan may be best
For we are still livid for attention as all men are
Jobs now secondary

Is Angela or Lisa tending any schlemiel on Sundays
Before more continental drift
Was more than water wind blown
It's hand to see past temptation
When what's in front of me is a still life
The one's Katrina victims felt so ravage

But doesn't gov't mostly abandon us
It's okay to slow down (Don)
It's okay to pay the price of scrupulous money heads
That tax us to the hilt
Till were covered with silk
Giving me this underground awareness
Now what was it we should do
Before spending air time shares
Maybe one day the tax on big bank
Bailout money will come our way
In the corner of this envelope, it says
"Sharing from the care of the Monoliths (Obama's) Luxury Bill."
Stamped with an iron Gonzo fist.

"Throwback (ties)"

The inhumane burden of work
Never lessened by a chastic home
As if I were fastened to a cleat
The roar of teeter deathless and deafening
Reassures me of some small rebound and ties

The simple things we praise
Meeting clerks and waitresses and waiting in check
Not very much tangible to talk about
Am I paying for my ancestors sins one or two left
And in death there is no schism
And in life I find little that's soluble
Sorting out an everyday blessing through a beaded sun
To find my own immortality

"nearby"

I sat on your sofa for two not closely enough
Didn't we look like studies in deprivation
Qualitative teen souls of yore
Your arms crossed purposely
Just one of your mores comes across
And I said we live below our means
What a family's stubborn eccentric trait
Is my love below my means
The one my mind talks about alone
Can you feel it's energy
Through a tempered spring breeze
It's sequence so spontaneous
Pushing up your erythrocycle count
Before senescence slows us
I keep wondering about you
Know that I'm nearby as a placed key

"Meeting me"

I tend to go halfway
With almost every endeavor
Succumb to my wit being mum
Suffused as a peaking sun through a cloud's hold

If I met you spontaneously
With the energy I have like I'm on automatic (cruise)
Charisma and tact would take over and our modes
I'd ask you about yourself and what you like to do
When you said, "I like sport and beer."
I felt as equable as midday wave
Flirting against tan lines
And you and me in tandem
The way our taint world is suppose to be

So meet me tomorrow
But first let me feel those tactile hands
Meeting me halfway again
Clenched to each other's delight

"call in urgency"

The winds in March steady and vibrant
Vile as our union now never to unfold as Spring
It's as if it has an undertow
Without an equable voice tonight
And you sleep errant as a cat's litter
Then you smile at my twisted wonderlust how else to find
    equanimity
As the wind howls into morning past 10:10
Disrupting patterned errands
As the post waits on a shelf
Maybe I should call you before becoming posthumous
Some love doesn't erode it's like the erected Recovery Act signs
Dated without query
And you with the Deery guy off of Rt 100
What little is left to enact
But to rebel against one's solitude
Who cares about hopeless encounters or intercepted text messages
I'll be told off again until someone lets me engender
If only a bartender's soft talk
But these heavy sounding movements of the air

"In Slum Villa"

That norco bum
Just an unconscionable word
Sorry I didn't befriend
I admired your proclivity
To live off the land like a bud
And little else to do,
They made you leave your public nests
But name stars before pawning trash
And used tools for cash
I just thought you were once
Proficient Joe
How I bet you rest in peace
On the most colorful plumonage
And I can't being to sum up my own
Wistful decline, who knows what's in store,
So I wonder like bums do

"Affected"

I live like a hole in a rug – so worn but I cannot frown for long because I have another day to try to be happy as my shirt reaffirms the orange movement. It became the engrossing avant garde bangeois. Not much in the way of fancies as I knelt in front of your black crochet thong. A silk net catching skin, as I ponder our duties. I touched your near shabby gelled hair thickened by sweat like malt to a shake, with elongated antennae those bunches so stoic, and I'm positively affected.

"Crashing to Costanzia"

Sometime con artist, untypical behaviorist
That Stein Brenner adores more than Blake or Bracer
He and his colleagues make fun of
Soft talkers and this muddled soup Nazi
His favorite motto is "Serenity now"
I guess so when his unwanted girl friend licked stamps and died
Marisa Tomei woke him up from his moping
Sitting in that lusty park dodging pigeon doo
Between all those diner visits
And picking up copy #-5475 of the New York Times
All this while Kramer is in some sort of morph
In his mind pining for Hollywood
What a group in pixel, they perversely petition Jamie Gertz and
    vivacious Terry Garr
Just how far can they take their hi-jinks
Or are they serious perusing each for personal gain
Didn't they go on philanthropic vacations fearing their return to
    the states
And what's with Kramer's philodendron styled hair
A friend caught him once in a furniture store adored by a bevy
    of beauties
But this costanza, a weird pro
His father a practitioner of stopping short in cars, a love – making
    gesture so impure
And who celebrates "Festivals" for dead comrades during
    Christmas
And Kruger and me still don't get the human fund
How many times did he, the others scream, "Jerry, Jerry" as if
    giving away used money
Hollywood names, is it acceptable

"The Other (Jesus)"

Oh, that Elaine
What a conservative Jew
Never showing any cleavage
That takes its toll on the wiener
As the toggle switch went both ways bi-coastal as N.Y. is
How do you like that prejudice
As I dream of yuppie buns and puppies
Jerry would inquire about their authenticity,
The left side is higher than the right
And that Sammy Davis Jr. look alike lawyer exclaiming firmly
    in court,
"Their mine and their real".
We salute all of you
In every premiere thing you do tally ho to Puddy to
I wonder what it would be like walking in your shoes
Or Traci Lords for all that matters and Pitt in earnest incognito
All their lives so cognitive as if their acting

"Treating"

It does matter how we treat children
Every time without division of self
They really do understand the world and us
They know we need them more,
In a couple seconds I looked away, left the room

London cried as he got hurt falling
Never relinquished from love
Am I guilty for a second of neglect
I guess I'll treat him to a Bubble Blast Mower
So I won't feel so bad

"Gilded one"

I really like you, still
You can't be swayed by the kindest words
Said only in poems
The wall you put up between us
The strongest elasticity only found in
Spiders
Because you didn't want to hurt me
This love I know you keep at a distance
When I look over a bay's edge
I'll only find a strangers effervescence

"Caroming to dissolution"

What will suffice
Before becoming senior
Rank less important than comraderie
The seagulls that swarmed around me in mid March
While I fed them from my car
Left for better climate
Maybe they went away looking anxiously
For a colony of the lost condor
By far a love criss-crossed railway tracks
To your home
Where you stay laying in abandoned silly pride
While I lose initiative towards humanity
The ratio for the sexes a figment towards connecting

"Timely"

Relationships splinter
Because of exhausting love
That suffocates
Count the ways so not unconditional
Ours dead frozen at winter
Love leaves you and rarely returns
But some come back to the doused flame timely
Knowing all is better
The sooner you come like smoothing warmth

"Getting to know you"

The things we learn
At inopportune times
Continually they weave like an artist's pencil
Like the gradual color of her hazel eyes a fantastic delineation
To find we feel so beleaguer begging for affection
Sometimes the smoothing of squeezed limes entices me
And to know children are the sturdy wool
Holding us together
As they slowly embark at a pace
Were felt to worrying about them even standing her
    begrudgingly
Next to nothing
Just as Chinese silk caresses my cold neck
Hopelessly addicted to rub one not even in a dream
And all I got was a briefing

The hind you get from authoritative types
Or from a wind opening up a car door in late February or March

"Tell me"

Tell me
How could I end up in ruin
Like depicted flats am wondering on waters
I can't name
Any bum's rap as if it was an everyday plan to do
Nothing
Now I have the economy to blame
And Marissa suddenly fluff
Behind her protectorate counter forgetting my call
Carefully deflecting me with words as if I were a fly
So as to not be baited tenderfoot
We might have some in common, tell me girl
I'm so weary of dealing in chaste confinements
They become exiguous
And you leave me exhilarated
As a chirping bird at dawn's lunch
Afraid of what you may say

"Beyond disillusion"

If I read past a number
I can't even name yet
Just to forget disillusion
Would it lead to an infinity
Or would I stop because of a siren,
Or on the edge of a cliff or moat
Would my soul find me and steal passion
Before the swords of Damocles
Succeed all
I have an affinity for the unknown
Was it just God's pretense or something else
You were primed in delight
Before dispassion was the rule today
To deal with a world so disingenuous

"What moments reveal"

The exceeding contretemps of today
Big as a shed full of feed that shadow us
Affording us little stuck pride
The way I keep losing today
Like the nature of gravity a hanging cloud
Holding mists and rain
Similar to broken alliances I've known
Thwarting humanity
Indian Gods may ring on high and loud
Over us in 2013
Some are saving survival hits and underground bomb-shelters
With ventilation
Have we become a nation of evil
Because there are the monolith elitists
Unable to share vast wealth
I'd rather have the health of a wise man
Divisible to all
And every embarrassment but not common as before
Defines me for tomorrow with unspoken courage
As I shed myself to you
Can I borrow something hot as a scored match
We lay tangled up and obscure
Before dawn blinks open an eye of envy
Harassing us from feel downs
Not bothered by any perplexity
That stain of life we keep searching for
An even glow, the polish look you reflect on pale skin
When so meone's settled in a room
As if you were an attracting candle that posters

"Fetching"

No man of fiber
Stays conclusive to oneness or arms
That's the sadness of being old fashioned
Richness rarely defined and fetching
Will someone might ask at an eulogy
"Who else did he know or converge on." Go into detail
Two hearts not in reply
Never fetter as a wild beast in volition
Counting his way to many dalliances lining the starstruck planet
Viable vixens, panting, waiting to party with Clinique piled on
Leading to a vitreous path and that haunts' mirrors
Until you're a hardly noticeable flicker

"Unseemly"

Jo, rangy as a leg of a willow
You always looked
Tack and at the same time haute
My charisma rarely stood in your way
How was I to dry the dampness
Out of your worn jeans from a frosty soda can
Wedged between your legs
You wore your jewels unseemly
On a sleeve and arm
Dried your denim on my lap
Before our shift, klutz
With a blush that wasn't rogue
You never told me what's all this hurt
Inside you about
You and I were the same
Trying to eschew maturity by diverging
Me and Flo now wondered
Just where did you go, did you make a dent
By being easy and free
You once called me harmless
Is that a nice edification for change
Just where did you saunter
Off to momentary to filch men
With lips the effluent ether
To an even handed service
So distinguishable as a promiscuous sky
Who dignified stayed proximate

"Carrying"

Unknown entities
Need a nourishment so contravene
Your eyes tell me – Heather
Ready to be ensconced convey
My vague words before an entitlement
We may never know
What waits on sheepish corners
For you and I to romp shamelessly
Toward mediocrity before painted strokes

"A warning"

Careless self-righteous drivers
Would you ride a horse without a bridle
So, don't impede my driving on Rt 422
Just because your in a hurry or hurting
Take the time to be courteous instead

"Brushing up"

The canvas of tomorrow
A blurred dawn
Like waking up
Or growing up too soon
I'm still naughty, but nice
Filled with woe or wonderment
Tomorrow as today
I'll brush the unknown surface
Like spiders in contrast do
Will I find you – for mindless contentment
Pulling on straps while you massage
That tighten muscle around the neck
These laminating words
My only consort to .....

"Now thriving"

Some thrive in the dark's cynosure
Behind the lighted stain of stars
These toiling crusaders we envision
So mesmerizing and beady
Some dwell in the darkness just to forget
Listening to the rhythm of Tweady
Some of us flourish, encrusted to a rolling joint
Cruising to engagements in black limos
Before time slows us to old age
Cementing these clingy memories
Hoping to be emulsified to a friend
Like baste to flavor
If it weren't for coffee houses
So I would bend your light before enervation
What is life if we end up empty handed as
Trying to break that festered cloud
Until we stood before rain like columns
Committed and wet
Because you had something to say
Before debauchery and dawn grabbed us

"Just look"

Dreams unwind to 2004
Just woke up to new holes
In old socks behind me and pant legs
They won't peer the destruction of the world's
Vast hollowness
So I just felt like I was clocked again
Just fill another Shock Top to the brim
Just look what walked in so bubbly, rubbing our thoughts so
    cleverly
Are we knee jerked owls cemented to every woe
And bystander, baby now can we go

"Enduring"

How do we endure without dear John letters or novelettes
This lack of kindness in times of yore
Their was little abandonment
It reminds me of unyielding drivers, dummy ghost riders
So blank to humanity and feckless
It must hurt when star power implodes
Proud portraits now ghastly as Shanty towns with sage brush
Filled with pain you share with a couch;
Others I knew with tight folded hands
As if their wedging in a coffin of splayed silk
The sands of time not like the "Days of our Lives"
And Jack going back and forth with Margo
Somehow enduring every bad test
The last hold I had
Was you between the mystic sheets tingled
They say the best is yet to come
But all I remember are your then thin legs
Trekking wayward
And now I transpire alone never mingling much
Tapping into your spite was the last straw
And what I want gnaws and gnaws

"Rain taps" and (purports)

The rain taps unevenly
Throwing a few tacks out of that glass jar continually
Beating like Johnny B. with murk or mirth
Decide, as I sit on a toilet seat
That use to be warm thru March's ruggedness;
Worse than the NCAA's (Bracket) theories
Ready to boycott agendas
Me I had so braggadocio
If I got up from my parchment
Passion would fuel the unbalance of our ages
When your officiously ambidextrous warming the regions
The taps can't offset this loose shellacked love so customary
As looming birds ocular to taste
Waiting on branches for the taps to break each one defiantly
    clear
Moderate as the living balanced to a few

"This guilt"

Sometimes I need to know
How inconsequential the world is
The problems wait like birds on empty feeders
So my heart rate is slowed
Would I then, get down and dity plenty
To see myself at peace finally
Or would I be forlorn and filled with guilt
Mine or by association
For lessoning my sacrifice to others so clingy
I gave so much to fortify and protect
Why should I then forfeit my own happiness and need dear
I live by own creed some might call sacrilegious
Maybe a James' is at the fork in the road called
Blackrock where black snakes meander
I like to rustle at life like the leaves
That filch looks
And then lay still and blissful
In a famous shoot in my mind
My skin caressed against silk pants
Prone to you and soft rose petals
But then I rose quickly
To not feel guilt or shame
But it's what I wanted to do
Until I felt a correcting hand
One that only angels could subdue

"Be still"

Not unlike my personality
To read about others
As if sensationalism was a gift to some
To divulge into temptation to stray
I can't begrudge to myself
Better to free thyself of everything
And be stolid like Buddhists
Don't they sit like rodents
But their hands cross
Concentrated, still like moss
Or unchanged hills below sweet summer sun
As if their dividing slush
Their way gives in like vapors
To a sumptuous life
Cycle by doing nothing pertain able
And if one or each cry comes
Never a weakness
But an awakening and new birth
Me and Lindsay lamented by holding hands
Somehow we met blessed and after soluble change
Night times wolf disappears into mirth so variegated
As ancient doors and knobs beg us
We pass into their insight
Why rob ourselves of the unknown
Riches of life, it's passion
The dogtrots of monoliths
Before starting gates and streaks
And the bumbly gait of dainty
Kari Ann freakily cool
Stumbling to foreclosure
Before finding her foliage

"Enlighten"

Thanks
For being behooved at
2:30 am.
Disrobed a heart's glitter rightfully
You didn't want to see me hurt
Saved timed time shined like your
Dirty blondness
Later, never
Tapped into the obscure
To make things lighter
They will never be today either
The fun we had together just sitting
Wondering innocently
About you and that symmetry
And you talked boldly in facts like thick type
Some words shockingly but you open up in a swoosh
Where I was afraid until we hugged goodbye twice
But you still grip me
Like a particle undissolved
More than occasionally even right now
As only a light wind mutters
Feel me softly, don't interfere
Hasten and walk below the surface
As if we went thru the rivulet toether
To find kingdom-come
A cause to many

"These rooms"

These endemic rooms
I use to rush home to
Built for shelters or escapism
Railways crisscross stations
Some on the underground
That watch travelers near
E. Missouri and even Phoenixville
Dens of decorum housing men
Where froth meets lips lavishly
For healthy retreats and touts
About the Yankees stardom or quests
This room wary as the skin of Frey's character
Now Frey moyer's has a nice repose
Even between the chatter a rustic ambience
They said George Washington
Was found schlep at Stoudt's inn,
Where ghosts lay
I've often wondered all the places
General chamberlain stayed at
Tending to in roll back before a great surge
But history is so embarrassing;
Between prohibition, wars, Presidents
And all their contempt
Still Schama writes in beautiful containment
As if the words flowed to a perfect in-land rivulet
Where you can't see for miles
Just wrinkled mirrors
Because I breathed on you for longer than a second

Affording my wishes
The dream in this room, kismet
Cascaded from my brain
Now I have to deal with the containment of their facts
Only rooms are essential to all failings
But then what am I related to
Their cornered diamonds with cut corners
And the guffaw of Craig on late night TV
Before curling my hand in a pen
Inexorably in the upstairs room
Ridded of a shrew
The only place I'm steadily in tow with
Beside the whispers of the wind
That's tracing my quarters

"Graving"

Pull away but not the same as the wind's
Centrifugal force
Thru trees leaving leaves swaying
Shed a skin towards certitude
Passiveness is not a virtue as behavior
Have these works shown
Growing exquisite as ancient parquetry
Wait for my influence to warm you over
More than twice
As the night's bending light
Subsides
Never leaving me precisely aware

"Tomorrow"

We use to not have to think or ponder any day
There was no poignancy to getting to tomorrow
Hands ran over it, naked
And then these routines
That now seem like unmovable sorrow that's mad
Why then think of tomorrow's cloak
Without a plot that keeps me
Death will still pluck you
Where God sits above
Probably on a diamond encrusted chair
Knurled on the arms with the whitest pearls, he rubs
Eying the peasants below that he loves
Pocketing our every fall
Passing on the valuable potsherd
As if it were tomorrow's recreation
Was the perfect weave

"Deana" (c) you know who

You are the eclectic angel
Who came out of heaven and space
To a faltering earth below
With a voice so silky, a face that instills placidity
And a little bit eccentric too
Her eyes melted you without purpose
Like a colossus doe in your headlights
That could even make a soft chugging sound
Thru the sagebrush and bracken
Now she's pinched to my elbows and rear
On a railway train's retreat
Looking charged even in repose whispering
Without needing replication
Because your beside me
Who'd boycott beautiful support
As I forgot what this was about, but total glee

"Nameless"

You could've been a model, a fastener for tomorrow
Now your just a model of inconsistency
Someone I knew; pathless
Lost in the morning dew
Could've been the face in vogue
Shown on a bus window in Manhattan
Or even a strewn on a throw
That blows in winter
Now I don't take my hat off to nothing
Except to dinner
And to hide a buttermilk roll
And then I think of the residual glow
From orange hawkweed
Giving off nature's blessing

"Someness" (Not for everyone)

We stayed the same
As our birthright entitles us
Passive mules do become united to
Were like fastened clingy knights of art
In living rooms
How often do we hear one say about family,
"That one begs to differ."
He always tried to start something
Just by being unique as Donleavy
With words as startling as robin's
Ina morning's remainder
We all stayed the same until marriage
That's what brothers say,
But I'm a bit twisted
And still their a reliable caricature
They may stay the course
Shackled to burdensome sameness
But I've got a widening view to all
The kind that Ivan had
To shake his world
Born on his own trait with no decimal point

"I'll be forgotten"

You lost everything
But still you pierce
As if you jagged your prey
You forgot I'm human, still do remember
Your pretense is not a continuance
To dance around this haughtiness
You'll forget me easily
Because of hatred after the revenge
Longer after I'm gone
And shame is divided by unholiness
Into the rest of my existence
I'll still feel compassion for someone like
You, but I'm downtrodden to
The basics of our life
The same now that were apart
Sounding as the triangular hole of a conch

"Constant

The dog I had
Life's real possession
Always loyal
Even nearing the end I helped cause
I can't say that about too many humans
Who foil time
Come into our lives briefly
And then like a willow bud on a blown wind
Crisscrossing directions
The way pedestrians do
Flippery on 5th Ave.
My dog was the color of hushpuppies
Had the eyes of Heather
Them so hated to her
My dachshund waited until I got back
From any pet store
With a pig's ear
To dangle between teeth
And dripping saliva to frizz the ends
I like how he looked up from
Having a bellyache and restless snores
Before blessed to euthanasia
Still constantly there

"Extended rooms"

It's as if I have
Roomed with the fustier
Waiting in dark rooms is suitable
For wine and men
Wrong light can cause spoils
Wedged into defiant behavior with a blue stocking
Until Byrne catches us and blushes
Shakes her head as if she's wigged out
Smiles as Patrick foils our night again
So gaily wicked trying to plummet straights
All that he could muster
Almost entices though were inertly in tune
Through the cloudy judgment of beer, also
Are Keith's blues and grays
It's a matter of choice after midnight
From an extended welcome if only in my mind
I wish you had come and that's wha ti told Chrissy

"I'm leaving too"

It's over
Our time to finagle, I'm leaving
Nothing to rankle about –
Giving me five seconds of skin
This embellishment of hells racking was so mean
Don't remind me of a past of swelled pride
We were a wrongful cast
Now maybe I can flourish
With what little I have left
I can smile at someone close
Not that our time vanished like a sun at evening
Before one vesper
Hold me to nothing but dismay,
That wistfully slops my cold heart
Even when it's over I'll hear the buggy
Condemning me

"Belch"

For five decades
Never felt or heard the belch of adornment
To fully satisfy
Sometimes it comes from Angela's hugs
Every servile host is just a fantasy
The undulation of ghosts
Watching clothes on a line dancing in a curling pattern
And all I hear is the belch so faint
Of a bathroom's values or pipes
The sound so full of listlessness and breathlessness
Like there's nothing left to entice
Morning's drabness I'll duck again
So when can we dwell without duplicity
As I hold a festive hen
You feign such scorn and then you smile
Waiting to go
So still now in bed
With a light belch of air from your lungs
Flexed your firm breasts against me

"Distinct"

I can't molt off parts as if I were an animal
But I like the meticulous groomed
Hetero / heritage
To not one or the other
Please come across our distinction
As if were newly distilled micro brew
I know you like swords and crosses for tattoos,
Jett's brow, Iggy's forceful energy
Did these people fall to earth like meteors,
Jenn did
So lovely we could grow a metastasis
And not be concerned
Death would not diminish what we had completely
Was like shining changing meters
And those eyes and scent landing strips
Hid over thin linen
Walking on a promenade
It makes me thirsty for a distinct kiss
Before moving to the bulbous area

"Seething"

Your not lethargic to them
Whipping up scenarios, mac 'n' cheese
How could something so fervid
Become a useless scab
Please release me from this condemnation
For I have been wrongly affordable
You don't show one ounce of compunction
Oh, how you will be cast down further
It might be too vivid his concept
But until then
I'm fuming inside

Del Louis

"Four words"

I've devised a pact
You could put in many a system of pages
Just four plain words
Four credulous creeds of passage –
Birth, pardon, living and suffering and especially death
And does any of this matter
Maybe if your Algren, Poe, or Chabon meeting
Timelessness
Before the usual pain sets in

"Rising"

The life we lead
For some so hard
For some as if they were ordained
Visions were trusted
But fame is fleeting
Pain waits at cornerstones
Where cobblestone is busted
For all the shirts I've shred
You must've meant something
As time is fleeting cost stuck in debris
And then we begin again like a bud on life's tree
When I'm with you the joyous boy rises again
I believe we could meet any crisis at hand
Now, it doesn't seem I'm coming out better
But whose to know at the enclave of a soul
The riches I've found even peering at the hazel
Eyes devising the world
Rising to the plan

"Where I sat"

The windows of exquisite café's
Where I sat near
The mind plays with searches
Between the safe boundary
Someone asks,
"What are you looking at,"
Shades and plants
Slited skirts defining humanity,
Of someone I use to know
Whose eyes could sear any playing field
The color of Bickel's Chips
I was looking for a glimpse of you Amy
Someone to tell specifics without any falsehood
Before I fell lonelier
By the sight of strangers splayed on sidewalks
All but one tactfully inept

"In Buddha's Arms"

Inside this rectangle called home
Embrace all thoughts with solitude
Like Buddhists with folded limbs instill
To find space or just the unknown
Slay the strife and dithers
Stay on the continual upending path
When you heart the tone of dissidence
Where cultures collide with unbroken wrath
And know you can't be weakened

"With Vigor"

I wish I could sleep
With someone with flexible ideals
When I'm cursed and ignored
And feel repulse
To be with someone whose hard, but tender
With a voice a little thread
I hope it's raining outside with resilience
Before the air becomes gooey
Cleaving to your charm
Oddly enough we rise to the occasion
Or God's reprieve with vigor
Tossing clothes aside as if there spinning
Thru a wash cycle
Leaving the V-taper thong on
Revealing those full gluts
As if my mind needs more thoughtless obstruction
Seen through the rearview the thrall thirsting
As if she were a vapor
But her lips thistledown
Over a darkened cobalt night
Freeing trepidation

"The stones"

In our recession
Or my time of dying,
Strummer's smile affording while he rests
These still diamonds in the rough
The early years as if it were "The Last Time"
Shining pearls in still grass
Or was it Marianne
And those landscape stages like them exceptions to the rule
Not quite readying for moss
Stones in the throes of God's adulation or Ronson's promise
Iron willed combatants even the drummer
Raging on
Rolling thunder forever as Zim is
Pillaging the hearts of children and the boomers
I was hooked on in 74'
With the mystic album cover of head shots; the goat for the
    ritual
That riff master wearing Chinese silk scarves
With every thrown vibrato
Making golden candles blink and flicker
Like the deals set evenly
The arts of the few and Chuch
That make the world go round
Giving me shelter
And escape

"Reaching"

We both are self destructive
As wayward as the sexes are
You with your drinking and anti's
But me to timid mutilation
Is it a weak reach to
Building blocks
When the least company
Is just a tinge
And those eyes eradicate sadness
Still as filled chestnuts
On a clear path
Where our cheeks met
A fading sun's impudence
And the wail of a few thrush,
Stumbling on their borders reaching

"What I wanted"

Would you trust
Buying alternate menus
The way we did that lone day
As our dutiful waitress trying to impress on her first day
Even sweeping so wholesome
Kay conversing about school and herself,
Sweet as syrupy shortbread
Was all I wanted
As her apron got in the way
What it was I wanted along
Leola
Better than any chip steak on a
Roll that girl that sunders to Westchester

"Presto"

Time doesn't ration
Feelings, it steals from the passionate ones
With a piercing
It isn't incumbent
To most individuals paper housed
What I forgot to say – today,
"Would you make a pact starling
Without being flippant."
Planning expectations investing in shared
Lifetimes
Before the incorrigibility of tomorrow
Every heart in a heist of time slaying even thought
Can you spare yourself to me
Before sorrow increases
And furtive time belches to a day's end
As the gallant one smiles, holding on
As if time holds us captive
Instead of he beat against it mercifully
Taut as primitive bait and tackle subdues us
Over tilting skies simultaneously over cast
That matter the least
Just a brushed stroke to indifference

"Them Stones (alternate)"

In my time of dying or growing
Had Strummer's smile
And these guys
Still diamonds in the rough
Shabby like shrubbery
The early years, singing "The Last Time"
Shining pearls in still grass
And those landscape stages and escape
Not quite readable for moss
Stones in the throes of God
Raging on iron clad and defiant
Rolling thunder forever
Pillaging children and boomers
With every timed rhythm
Every dial set
Hot as a candle's flickers
Giving us all a glimmer of fabulous art

"Blurring"

I only see you
As a blur before or after awakening
A long last cast into a sea
Your bewilderment is fascinating
Now corrupted by minors traipsing around
I see us now maybe blasé
With no presence
Singular as a cup of coffee
With steam so blurred and translucent as you
But I like the blur of a light's tinge
Brushing against the shadow of trees across every foyer
Thin as the outline in my mind with no outcome

"Softness"

"I've been construed by others
To be mellow
Easy for infringed upon like waiting pigeons
Come pluck my ear
You to may become aged
If niceness ever sets in tell me a little
Sharing kindness ot measure softness
As if it were shares of cotton
In an outdated world not ever aided by one stranger
I see a common pleasantry to belong
The way a plug skitters along it's ribbed surface as trout descend
    deeper

"Exemplar"

It's become
Habitual to be like them
Reciprocally basking in hurt that never shows
To accept being lonely
Without caring
I can't
I can rebound from who I am like a sentinel
And know I can learn
From someone a little different
I didn't make up here one name
Whose just as mad and nomadic as me

"Before the First pitch"

Coincidently
With no reason
Except Maryland's midsummer heat
Following an enticing thong
Enthusiast
To the aged, warped boat deck to sit
One built for despair
Small cruisers swerve in the brine air
Near this inland bay looking for a base
Rocking the brine waters before Phillips Sea Food
And I have nothing much to say
Before the ceremonial first pitch
As if I was shipwrecked with Shrek on Neptune;
Lost in the moon time of heightened desires and riches
I put away a lasting expression of steady comfort
That embossed card in my loose pocket
You gave me
Beating against the sun
Before you said, "call, we'll see after tomorrow's
Nine, I'll let you draw the line."

Del Louis

"What I'm telling"

Who am I to tell you?
What you are
All the truth is double edge sharp
Tied to time and fractions or even space
Wall street may've heard that to
Until a harp player from heaven arrives
Half trùmping the evil there is
A forgiving face for some arrives
But steady to the bow
A smart person knows I'm not perfected
To the minor miracle for long
Was just a slick trick of tomfoolery
Even if we have a gift that's strong
Projected for tomography or sainthood
But whatever is ever
Faithful as you
Once was your better cause
Forging happy memories
Now what do you expect me to do
Split like Jim and tomboy Jenn
Maybe the truth is sped in reverse
When back in time pilgrims were bankers too
One's name was Tom
There I said the trick puzzle word again
Before getting on God's green
Still a heal for tongue lashing
Tied to patriot ideals
Weened on not taking sides
But I'm telling you to endear
Is to accept ruggedness of
Anything
Always have

"Dread"

I didn't know
What work meant
With its shabbiness
Caused by routine
I now know I need the dread of
Work
It is my servile pig
Without it I'm not led
To a tinge of serenity
Or the light freckles
Of your face doyen
You see it even heckles the
Upper class

"Waiting"

I always put things off
Sometimes they become more broken
Ask our leaders
Is a working mind a hubless wheel?
I also always put things off
However is this the way to affording change
Or to feel more hurt by delay
Liable as a growing wart
Maybe I am part leprechaun
Needed as a libertarian joyless
Soon to be maxed out
Intruding to all this procrastination
Waiting for you

"The Sunset Girl"

As I was in a deep meditative state
Just talking, enter
Linda
You were cool as menthol
Medicating my soul
For the future and all loss
It was better just to know you
You were oozing, slightly inebriated
Beauty inundated
As you casually walked those stairs
A blonde caterpillar slinking
Trying the vamp routine
In front of your sister and me
Still I wonder about your beauty
Never finding if it was valid
Or a sling
The last time we passed
Mute admiration at Covatta's

"Why talk" (of things)

We don't talk
You listen to the silence
Of your nature
My occasional real voice
Just fills you with anger
The dreaded truth spilling over
Like fire spreading
As if someone made a bad choice
Why talk in continuance
When one is lonely

"Dreamless"

I use to stay awake
Thinking I would miss something
Like a brother I knew
Who never came home
But I thought aging was necessary with
Sleeplessness
Life was provoking us
The things I had to endure
When I was young
I'd try again a thousand times
Until I learned the prick of desire
Is a waning wick
For their only is assuredness of one man's plan

"True Blue"

True commitment so blush
Allows us thoughtless unseemly moments
Of twinned equability to others
Not exceeding Gladwell's converse someday
We pick people, places, or things
To set us apart
Never remonstrant to change
Name one life that has a complete regulatory mode
As Frank Wright's
I'm not making timid excuses
While in repose with relaxing agents
As hands and limbs liberally roam to a muse
True commitment
Bound to the joyous tether
And my dull surroundings
I come back to every time like an assailant
Even after a tepid rain falls
As if it's bolting me down
Truly unacceptable someone else's
Rendition
Of what they want me to be
To possess the world I falter from

"Silent"

This night is so still
Here in April
Not one tingle in rustic pipes
No drone of planes
Macerating clouds over Glasgow St.
This must be similar to a rapture
Before raucous joy
Or nature comes undone tomorrow
By whistling Northern Central
And the polarization of leaders
Soon grass and poinsettias
Will star at our still life,
Peculiarly
Begging for water peacefully
Blind to our dumb thoughts

"Hag"

Once there was a pre-teen girl
Who lived on the next corner around Zwinter
I think her name was Leah
Her mom was racked from previous drug use
But the clincher
Was when someone said she clicks her heels
Incessantly like a hag in first person
I saw this one day walking my dog;
He didn't care he hustled along pavements and shrubs
She wore black and was going
Clickety click, clickety click
Running goose bumps down my spine like spiders
I thought she could line me with measles or the plague
So I looked away without helping or crashing the curse

"Placidity"

I placated you learning
An admonishment of sorts
Even though were still together
Like a speck of parsley in a bowl
A weave in an incomplete pattern
That looks strained and shoveled
And then with savvy as you paw
My shoulder
Finding something to revel in
Playgoer, sightseer
Inventing a sense of placidity

"Tranquil line" (To perfect)

In my musty shambles of a study
Held to trying to master little domain
As if I'm trading skins
And what's more relevant
Than losing time and direction
If I'd ask a 100 people certain questions
Would I find the same answers
Or words dancing to explicit poems
Sorting a messed life
And the ghosts of a troupe imagined
Some happily sounding in a stoic head
Sometimes
We address our basic needs pass food, water, shelter
With the likelihood so tranquil, it's line
Above a deep blue sea
Where seagulls race
Or below consciousness
Where someone is moved by the deep ones
Needless to fight off this transformation

"Prowling Devils"

It felt as if I was staking hearts
When I saw a cop
As I was turning onto Prince St.
Before reaching the intersection's top
I felt I hit the cul-de-sac
And then turned around and left for home
Passing my pavement
Lights flashing behind my car in red
While I was already in my door
Checked my plates then he left abruptly
My heart racing
Now drunker laying on the floor laughing
At a foolish stunt
So ever defied beneath
A part in a play
Where few can stay outside these margins

"Once a river of peace"

At first early on
You were by chance
Beauties deception
A river of peace my charmed bracelet
You open up portals
We walked or paddled to
Too powerless finally to welcome change
A river of peace unmatched
Love past sunsets and gravel
A space at it's mouth
I could never drown in
Because your arms stretch
As if it were a place where kids
Sheepishly play
And then you let go
So rife with lust
For fear of being one
Contrarily mine
I scrambled like dice
For any reason, still do without asking
Why
Let you bask in continual shame
Finding another conveyance
Douching me far away
Trying to find a semblance

To that river of peace again
Was I the eyelet for passed rope
Until that river dried
Fragmenting futures
But then I could see past
The graying mist
Only a glimpse
Like cigarette smoke
Or from a Monte crisio 4
In a pond filled with summer's algae
And little gleam
Now knowing I made no rippling effect

"Ingenuously"

A moment
Before regaling your friend or lover
You walked past me and those pine chairs
Like a Raven retreating
From old refuge or compost
Your eyes on me refuting something
What if I had sat
Next to the blonde
At the table beside you
Made the most of surreptitious meetings
Before a waiter's arm flails
Over a receptive menu,
Just tell me, "what were you thinking"

"Entertaining Loss"

Downsized by the strong magnates
It sounds like a bulldozer's blows
Monoliths who continually divert
Move funds before bail outs without margin
Squashing us like weak birds in incubators
These strangers who didn't meet quotas stayed
So they use the term economize above greed
Before firings and lies as if they were traders
Wise men say save something
For when you return to work or retire
But it seems like a small death
Having nothing already
When you looking for love on routine
Whilst I need those quirky funds
To aspire when living suitably
Before a gratis, quiet departure
Some waited for
With widening grins
As if they were etched in stone
The guiltiest pleasure
You accuse me of
I've never held briefly
The times we weren't in tandem
Many not closely
In the new millennium

Perfecting failings
Aroused by night times pulse
Unrehearsed portals of escape
The nicest ones taking that plunge
Feeling someone's euphoria
In your presence
Or sitting beside (Eve) at 1:10
Even when honest is euchre
Never realizing being guilty
Is the summation of longing weirdly
Something wholesome is dissolving with
Division as two halves can't haphazardly share
I can't feel guilty over many acquaintances
Now lost, frozen as the tundra
Not even caring for their meteoric charred remains
On an earth's crust barren of regard
Some sort of comparison remains

"Limits"

When I was younger
I stayed so lurk within limits
As if I was a sardine
In it's custard
Hiding in a shiny metal tin
All those should house a 60's Mantle card
Instead in cellophane
It's as if I'm not wanted much
Even if I were a finished fish
Sometimes there is a lull
Behind everyone's darkness
Your hair thwarting shadows
And dim light
Resting in my arms
Your breasts cower, smile,
Cradled on a bar's rolled top edges
As I stare at an old Benson and Hedges ad
And a pile of filed, clean beer glasses
Waited to be moved after rush hour
And the sweep of darkness
Without a relaying message
Except Dani's sardonic grin
That's graphically insuperable
As her surroundings

"Curio"

Laying in heat
In humid garage walls
Insects pasted like kid's stickers, some
Beating their tanned wings with savvy
Mine in an ice claw dangling
Flat lined to deliver once seldom anew
Eschewed far into this new millennium
Pleasure now derived in milliseconds
When you brush my mind willingly
With curded words
Painting tomorrow's portrait
Of what we always do
A current to new renaissance

"Constructive"

The art of helping young lives in
Construction building a plan
Like guilt of pleasures
Their so innocent
When I to am straddled by own perils
And daily insults mounting
Strewn to their color
And happy changing foliage like
Maybelline colors
Now knowing at last
How to be constructive

"Flowing"

Deprivation
Never stopped me
From trying new things
Even at my lowest pointed depth
When all have regularly abandoned me
The biggest form of deriding
When I slowly came back like a natural ebbing flow
I left everyone I knew
I became a guru to every stranger
Then adopted a piece of them too, lost to a past
So hairbreadth that waning guttural cackle not of birds
But now the ebb flows
Below the buttress of our knees
Smiling at this action now whose pigeon holed

"Steady"

The ride of tomorrow
Unknowingly the sky of today
Like shaving cream
Or Elmer's paste trying to dry
Under graying construction
Paper molding or unballasted
As my own existence
Shipshape as a tired wayfarer
In North Africa's sun
Up ahead he made a circle in the sand
Weaving curious love that's not endemic
Somewhere someone takes a man's hand abetting
To cure her wickedness
But he only looks away
Patterned as Keith's nose thumbing
Irrelevance
Touching al our graying's hearts
Sometimes steadily they accrue
An everlasting hue

"We the deep"

To the deep thinker
Who feels trapped and bottle-necked
By lack of indifference
In the world
With pained expression and then joy
We sometimes, we the deep
Can't distinguish between what we want
And what is
In these bars of knowledge were revealed
But not the tomboys or their gender

"Understand this"

Surely like most
I want to know
About things
I knew nothing about
Like fancy watches
Before those hands are strewn
On a closed faced Movatta
To test intelligence or skill even fishing
Can be alarming and a detriment
Even without a cell phone
God forbid getting snagged by a dinner turtle
Knowing when to play the slots on time
A Motorola pager may list
Injury and scratches for football
On any given Sunday
And still I find all love
So onerous, but not the sounds of
Zydeco and alternative
I latch on to
But Katina at (Como)
I know nothing about, still

"Bare Essentials"

Genes with their inherent and
Inherited risks
Similar to invested life
Once golden or rarely met
What one doesn't infuse
Is lost and stripped
When looks or riches wane
Like a San Diego sunset
Forever searches and reaches a transformation quickly
Without us
The particulars of niceness
Found
Even in Zenyatta's nod, Antony's voice
Now past the worries;
That he or she said,
"Is he finally gonna leave,
Is she explicitly gone,"
Props in games of choosing
Diss me for plagiarizing about the man
Yes recent plans, events
Have changed the current picture to a sad influx

"Who says for certain"

Who says life has to make sense
Look at fastidious monkeys
And Aristotle
Who probably dealt in perspective
And Descartes whose numbers
Probably fell closer to truth
Do the numbers lie
Stuck against loss so decadent
As for the young strawberry blonde
Debutante, Oprah or someone help her
Her freckles have aging spots
The ones who say life has to make sense
Maybe I'm aware of their longing or
State so solitary
Still even at this time
I'm a contradiction of sorts
Yet in my own class yep
Except for the ones I call the few
Might know
The pains of being a rambler
A study in defying loss or gain
And I'm told I'm one who jumbles
Questing to Frost's circle
Who says life has to make sense
Fools who won't beat their wings,
Over and over as if wincing

"Variables to Choose"

Do you think sameness
Befuddles good judgment?
My friend envies accompanying boredom
From stolid 2nd dates
Lesser than imagined sex
From varied customers we've met
Along the curtail of time
No, were not the johns
But Don Juan waning theorists
Enthused and derived from the same bond
An endogenous need before declined to senescence
The eye of every beholder
To thrive on variety thrice
The customary insult to most who are once born
Nice portrait in their spheres
Licking salt peter
Cletching the black jaw of loneliness
But I'm not like them bolted to denial
And resentment forever
I'm sworn to an assortment of loose gems
And the fervor of suicide fems

"After I'm gone"

Is death
A conclusion
Like every unmarked cul de sac
Is death
A foreground of
What a mired life couldn't erase
Are we just an eyelash
On the blip of humanity
Death usually allows no discord initially
And is finally freeing
As wind swept leaves
Curling like mini-flying saucers
Traceless as burned coal
Out of our sight
Now his, her life a blur
Cause we must soldier onward and question
Death is black always or not
But we can unveil truths or half truths
About the afore mentioned
As time speed son like Calvin on the rail
With that canny grin that engages loyalty
Someone asks,
"Why are we here if we've accomplished nothing." Really these
    are points for professors

I silently think, to be stoned or mocked
But not by a living God no one can see,
But feel his rush, look at nature
Folding
And these churches in Connecticut
Along curt passage ways
Now leading my mind to Charlotte's
Breathless hugs and kisses
That I miss at 7:59
But back death
I t doesn't humble the living
Of those who don't give quarterly
I just wonder, but not in vain
What someone will ask
After I'm gone is death just death
Or are we still being tested by words
The embodiment of every soul reaching

"Forgotten"

Spare me the sharing
Hitherto to more loss
That accosts like an intruder
How could I not be happy
On this day of May
Seeping like chocolate syrup
So bright and sunny orange
Well, that's what the depressed do
That bright color
And it's blindness to some, cold realization
Could be the black cloak of death
Surrounding even calm waters so glossy
That look like sheets of glass
Struck by nature's evil forces that
Belch
Before anyone could ask why
And then become like me
More forgotten
Than the blue sky of today
That waits to instill
A favor from you

"Jigged"

If memory serves me well
Like dim sconces thru passages
Of the whacked
We pensively reflect upon as a jig
Thoroughly trounced nearing our knell
The spurious monkeys disconnecting life
Not wanting interrelation but control
Made me
A wild hyena in discord or limbo
With an interminable need to grow and bear
Imagination just the precursor of
What we believe can be
The fruit of it's dispersion
With change as relevant as the seasons
Becoming a muse before maturity to all
Fawning for the same glam dream
Seen in yesterday's Rockwell
Just a minion in our bidding wars

"A part of me"

I'm glad you were in my life
Kept me straight and streamlined
Too late to take things for granted
Never did much anyway
I'm glad your still there
I wonder if you think I've ripped you off
You did it to me to, Dad
With words like cold sharp steel
Pressing inward to the skin
Some retort in silence
I can still see the abrasiveness , when
Visiting your cut gray stone
I sense your still living inside me
Brushing that laminated spot warms me
Hoping with thoughtlessness
That I was your equal
Now no better, are we
Then a thin blade of grass strewed forever

"To feel rage"

If there is controlled rage
It's what keeps us going
It to reaches a point of calm in our hearts
I don't know it's relation to pain or
Loss anymore
It's ragged, hapless edges
Brought me to you
In a general meeting of safekeeping
Never jaded by nice talks
Unto morning's dew
Refreshed love's onslaught, raging thru

"Timelessly bound"

On these sun filled yesterdays
Slighting our dissolution
Sipping orange-aid or ice tea
We really did puree the purest thoughts
Straining at bird – feeds and the and the poplar
Turning that miniscule hour-glass upside down so repeatedly
Trying to hold time down
But it just seems to purge beggars
That wait at the seam
Of their own knowledge
Like the ones on this unemployment rope, bound
Dangling pride remonstrate to failed systems
Wait for money to hold time
Briefly concurrent not changing a thing
Now waiting for the final jig
To extol even Goldman Sachs
What wrong-doings
May be called extenuating circumstances of the pomp
Leading to a portent towards apocalypse without reward
That cool breeze on a hyacinth
A lost trail leads to you beat and transient
More at home on merging Greyhounds
And lanes that disappear
As my eyes close to a milky kiss
That thwart congestion
On another millisecond trek

Del Louis

"Look outside"

Everything outside yourself
Is within your silky sleeve grasp
It glistens, yes it's true
That hidden elusive quality,
Cramps, object from fear
It's inside you divinely
Found from all suffering
Burns a heart like a rose so new
So, why didn't you tell me
Before nature erases us, look outside
That wall of pride to find me

"Rugged heart"

Who bears an unwanted child
Stays awhile and then deserts it
You were ruthless then
In your world
Not quite ready
Or curled to a pattern of life or
Rustication
You can't just come back
Like a shiny boomerang or lost guilt
Now she's roughshod
To unshared opinions as anger stays
Can't pray to Mary
She didn't get her way or much love
You were so young building your own domain
Your daughter took comfort in the insane ones
Boy, she must feel some sort of foreclose
The kind most get in middle-age
But your rugged as a claw
No words to ease a rout
You shout to defy the curse
Because you had the charisma
With the sweet rose water look
At thirty, sparsely kindred
Now not shuffled by hick-back gears
Or ten inch nails
Steadied by Mike's finger on the right key
As your voice trails off
In a nicotine swallow

Balanced by his up man ship
And the untimely s mile of his,
Tomorrow's yoke, a knotted truth unties
In the spare rooms she keeps him
Close to her heart
Closer to her rugged heart
Where all doesn't have to be stormy
Close to her rugged heart
Where all doesn't have to be stormy
Close to her rugged heart
A soothing kiss
Like menthol in air comes whistling
Never was a search hound needed
She simply doesn't care what you think
At the edge of the bay
Barefoot, sitting on a crag
Listening to you (mom) and the sea
Waiting to scathe

"Soulful"

It's as if they embattle a foreign cause
Against me
As I'm now quite reciprocate
To everyone's selfish control
They must see me as a physical embodiment
Of nothing
Try to enlighten me
With a smile so soulful
The ones you see on tourist signs
Tell me if you can of words
With a freeing compass
To bring about a change
Not defined by boundaries
But simple sharing,
Rangy limbs like caterpillars
Bending before darkness
Becomes our unknowing
Self edging along
What becomes even more startling
Souls walking in that little space
Of marked tombs, searching
Outside nature only scratches the
Surface
For every plan
Some kind of ruin or passing plan
When I see you I'm revered
Time stands still like in June
And I still feel you lifting me
With every gimmick
What an exciting g-force
Now revving up to balance

"Speeding to Nevermore"

Not quite reaped
For being benign
So few participate to solidarity
Couldn't get you thoroughly in my realm
Love's too painstaking dull
Maybe I just didn't try
Now you never appear in that place anymore
And I seldom come in to check or socialize
Beside Dani's dry humor
Can't seem to find
Someone whose not lackluster
After the last call and snuff
I hear a whisper before a snuggle
Dressed in your feminine glow
Starting a mild, nice come-on
I hope tomorrow it doesn't pass

"Prodigal one"

You said you wouldn't be bored
Even by remoteness or jail
You have no regression in aging
Even with Depps' reminiscing
Rendition
In a barren enclave, of Nellcote
Mastering open (G)
Threading the grooves to a needle
Carrying the greats defying all logic
Defining art with new wrinkles
Where I haven't begun to steadily cop
My own need to transform
Is a pressure that implodes
Saved by the prodigal one's vigorous
Never berating sound
Freeing the mind's cage
Like ether or Ava's
Steely mesmerizing eyes that draw you in
My regards similarly characterized in
"Casablanca"
Where would I be
If I couldn't find counter balance in
Haunts
Somewhere between a circus and the timeless
Wallenda's gig
Maybe jugged like a gypsy for a day
Beside a moth that never leaves
Cupped in it's own confusion

"At the Hillside"

Reading about the cold-blooded murders
Of the likeable Levan sisters, at work
Their way to death so unreasonable
And beyond anyone's realm
Left up to a hook and the devil's wide influence
I wonder what was their last overwhelming thought facing this
    misanthrope
When a bullet becomes someone's elixir
And then emancipated by God who knows all
To the living another murder by ellipses
Where every sloping esplanade
Has the shadow of a closed lens erelong
Of something we can't comprehend

"Ode to London"

My lovely little sprite
I bargained I didn't need you,
All thought was similar to following
An invisible wolf pack
To a den in hell, what did I come to believe
The bad looks better
When immune systems restore us
To rationalize loss after the pain subsides
We do; somehow, when
If ever a true calling
By (God) shading him from disaster, my son
When you walked alone ¼ of a mile to seven eleven at three
    o'clock
I thought you were gone forever
And then when child services intervened
Due to a careless misunderstanding by broken parties
To neat misremember is hodgepodge
Worse is repetitive nauseous thinking
I'll never see those pale, puppy-like bulbous smiling cheeks
I'll never see these burning chestnut eyes
That adore trains and pop-pop or blue-berry pop-tarts
I thought what kind of guardian is he (who) comes first
Before that adorable boy (London)
Who likes to hang in my arms like a slowed propeller
I thought who is gonna feed him raw carrots he loves
I might never again see him strut purposely like a mummer

Then like a wind of change bring him back enforcing counseling
Now I can tell him he's cranky pushing his cars over oak tables
As he echoes those words back
Now he can tell me over and over, "Let's play nighty-night."
That's when I let him play with cosmetics and lotion
Sometimes we pull covers over tightly, and he say's,
"Close your eyes."
And lately a wispy, "I love you." To grand-mom too
All this from a child who understands our world silently
But still too little to tell us
With Sesame Street, Dr. Seuss, and sprouts for trusting neighbors

"These waters"

That still glassiness tries to mire truth
On the river almost quite solemn
Like the water in those kid's clear globes with portraits
With floating stars
It gives insight to our souls we reach for
But when a light wind blows;
The waters throw crisscrossing karate chops
Breaking those pristine thoughts
Lastly our wants almost futile
That spirit on the water
Means were not alone
As the white brakish foam races
Lines our toes on the inlet's shore

"Thick and Thin"

Life makes us contradict
Our true feelings
Always elusive to change
I found you indirectly, thinly disguised
Charismatically made my point
Is it a dicker to lose
But you held on indelibly
Not knowing if I was incumbent
To something else, someone
And if you were caste
It wouldn't matter a bit
We've shared more than malt
I'm confident to be your choice
Was once so thinly spread
Now I'm your rare find

"Holding time"

Time with it's moments so pleasing
Cutting through your every dull confined spaces of the mind
As if searching
Like a speeding hurricane challenging us
With no underplay but frailty
All this wasting thought on hold and what if's
You could've told me something
So I boldly go past all wreckage
Twisted debris like the limps of a ballet dancer stretching
To other reaches of my heart so deft
Finding a hand you took crossing Angel and that floor
And every tireless gay stranger
Some that can't warier or spurned as I was tingling
And I can't stand
Being alone every sheepish night without a kindred conquest
Dawns on tomorrow's unknown plan I left
But every where I look or turn I met
Just a cause to reflect on nothing, but a
Solid reliable, and trusting bond that's good enough
My time with you to ascend those feelings
Reaches that turning point happily against skin so moiré
Careless and unconscionable to passing time

"How could you"

How could you be so uncaring
Bringing children into this unloving world
Beset by protestation
Against everything that's good curled to this madness
Little ones need mothers to be
Thoughtful acting protagonists
Instilling a nearness but then you withdraw
To the need of a man
Holding them in higher regard
Without knowing the truth of what their about
Another life with no outlook
But to fawn your vanity to mirrors and all
Is it better for them to be drown babies
Oh, God how could I ask such a favor
I didn't want them to feel hurt so directly
Falling in a world lost with no longitude
I never wanted them to feel so much pain
To foster all this regret in those teen years or later
Just maybe it isn't all pseudo
When becoming tomorrow's lone laureate
One said, "I don't need her, I can stitch my own path."
Whilst some indignation never ends completely
I hope her wrath becomes solvent
See it spritz like a falling star at night
Giving me one glimpse of redemption

"Remember"

Remember, try
When the soul you can't see
Becomes too intense like boiling lava
And life is surely too hard
Know nothing can penetrate our love
Even when u needed rebuking
Or when I was chasing shadows
Only one man is reasonably sure
What we might do tomorrow
Please remember me, as if in shared
Humanism
To huddle to your family, make a plan
Because time will surely hunker me down
As all treasures are laid to rest

"Creeping to exits"

Afforded outlets to outlets
How could I ever be bored
A solitaire for her
Air Jordan or Adidas for him
Am I just chasing away pain,
It's not plaster of Paris
Buying more designer clothes
On fancy whims
Maybe I should be growing sorghum
Running out of outlets now
The way of Wendy O'
They'll soon take the sulfur out of lights
It's so hard not to stay supine
In a life that leads to such misery
Without a dog named Toto
You need all kinds of wizard try
I worked so hard and my plowshares got whacked
Now all I do is speculate about you
As if we were floating, pasted
In a celestial body
But I'm just a pleader
And your not my friend anymore
No use in venting nobody hears
A t twined thought as if it were eerie

"Swept by the breezes"

What would've it been
To be savvy Mark Belanger
Chasing down scorching liners
Off Hillerich and Bradley bats
As if they were un-mined ores gathered
This record breaking Areole of yore
I wonder if Bouton saved him
For a spot in his books, beside Robby
And why does this Cardinal
Stay in this desolate town, it's just a finch
It's so hard to fathom
One that Dylan hasn't yet found intrusive
All that we filch we decidedly come back to
But sometimes that greatness cannot be filled
It can only be finagled by paper kings with
Asterisks – for remembered greats or whose
Time is coming

"Plausible ridges"

Driving and grazing
Over all these countless ridges
Along New Holland roads
It's as if they engulf me
And every thought I had of you
Spoilt with little or no collateral
I said I would always love you
But that was a long time ago
Even nice guys can't be faithful
When painting our portraits
Don't use the excuse of being hung out to dry
I toiled so hard in labor
I needed someone's abstract point of view
And still you curse me,
Twice I saw your ridges
Beside the warm glow of fire
Your hands crossing zealously
What are you transpiring to
Traversing buttocks moving parallel,
Rarely all ridges yield to nature
As the yearling begins to firmly pace
And then I rolled over the ridges
To where the snakes lay low

"Ricochet"

You see a round pretty face
The look of Playboy or Vogue
I like em slightly slutty
Thinkin she could curb lasting fear,
Possibly,
Soon you would be in her
Comforting sphere
As young pristine love turns rogue
Sour as a sweet tart
Even if it's color is blue
After the exquisite random sex
You dreamed of
Or the first kiss so full of spontaneity
It's usually downhill
Ricochet as rain on that white spout
Where you stood idly waiting debased
Like a batter on a split-finger fastball
Did I squander another as if they were
Sputum
Sitting at home alone
Balanced as a ricochet
Straining to see tomorrows

"Edging"

Cold wind in May
Quivers on a bridle in Louisville
The edge dawning on equines or man
Two almost dead pan
Speak of lifestyles so dearth
As if being drowned by small failures
Mock-heroic before early summer
Where plenteous dahlias smile
Hanging against the loggia's
At the premium outlets
Where modernization
Is okay in a modicum
I wish I could hear your voice of reason
Scant reminders that I'm okay
Preparing me for change and tomorrow
With an orderly edge
As if I borrowed wisdom
From every shading cloud, edging away
Succinct to our own metaphysics
Each casual plan flickers

"Searching"

If for once before searching
We are kept arm chaired by sports
Or held by desire's pleasure
Below a moon's crest, shimmer
And then suddenly
When that spark of desire
Initially fades like on ember's waning spark
Measures us
Do we accept anything less is gambling
You could slowly build that fire inside me again
Would I be satisfied then without tutelage
With what I know now minus a compass
Scantily clasped to the silky layers
Of a thinning happiness like cows in old pastures
Would I simply move on, like a brushed stroke
Of a wind's Zazzy sound almost bereft
Or accept all wreckage
Affording the clashes of the sexes
With the demure smile of a lamb before sacrifice
Lastly embracing God

"Nina"

You real understand me
Simply just your acquaintance
Healthfully entrenched to my soul's bend
Telling me what to tell her,
One who never lies
All that tender converse at the bar
What good are we if we can't ask favors
Of many shapes and coloring tomorrow
Coated to this denial
And those hazel eyes
I can't swim safely, freely from love's debris
You planted the mind's moon
Near the river's edge,
Unwinding these spoolet thoughts are running freakily
Why do things stay so ephemeral
Until you bequeath me
Waiting on that dark, steep macadam
Where that hotel overlooks us
With it's cheap masonry
Assuading comfort
Beside your lighted cigarette
Burns like an indefinite star
That times every move

"Feed the outrage"

The fads of tomorrow before thievery
Are they minute posterings
Fanciful things not yet approved
By the squares, freaks or the masses
And how can we predict then
Which ones come back
How can we reproduce
Howdy doody, the clown prince
And that wimp pee wee in tight suits
The craze put forth by such famous
Innovators without traps
Lydon, Richards laughing at the posers
With a sense of normalcy
Why is it a trend to repeat ourselves?
It isn't a failure to not move on
Not all are fakes, but true worshippers
The same fan that would bear your cross
How Pitt must've remembered Redford
And Blanchatt, O'Sullivan, O'Hara
But Lindsay a crooked jewel
Outlawed by her own normalcy, demons
By which there is no media standard
Little runaways on the devil's casting couch inhaling lawlessness
Dying fat just turning to lard tied to the insupportable lanyard

"Before crumbling"

Being completely ignored
Even by strangers we adore
Casual reminders of an enduring future so cryptic
I thought hell rose to meet the earth's floor
Steered to gravity
As if cuffed by a strong wind
Even crumbled feta before disintegration
Reaches us creamy and ingested
But crumbling wilting flowers once silky
With their faint reminders of beauty
We croak forward to
Like frogs lapsing on dry moors
As their waning scent so rich
Slackens before crumbling
Vaguely ward to the soul
All this matter to be your mainstay
I can't reinvent
Is it just a whirligig
As I rumble thru your hair and creased skin that quivers
Like a dying flame in shadows
You held on to the end
Or the end of something seemingly
Remote, why
Even the worst love has no rational

Thinking
From where I sat sinking in my own
Despair
Where Eve's eyes broke the pain
Sublimely without words
In every silent surmise
I could never crumble
To lost passion and intaglio hearts
But broken chips of Oreo's;
I can tip in a milk glass
Never quite knowing which way is down
Tomorrow like Obama today
Try owning up to failures
As if their self-inflictive
Rallying cries

"Wavering shadows"

This tide so like nature steadily
We cannot thwart the truth
We never fully can discover
What Aristotle meant
That movement fluctuating to a fastball
Just like swept feelings
Goose eggs on a scoreboard in Kansas City
All those who came before
I can't tuck away; what is it about (one)
Joan and Schleps we lovingly embrace
Holding on to sorrow that divides us
Cowardly to not say, "I'm sorry." …
But what the f… raking a clean sweep
Are we still children caught up in a time warp
Staring out at a sea's thoughtlessness
Needing jiggling shin of bikini clad intruders
Who'll sit on a bed's edge perfecting a night's tone
With Margarita's on the rocks
Fake humping with their slick thighs
Just similar to a tide's thrust breaking
Locked into a line with buoys
As perpendicular as the way you lay
With a torso spread, squinting eyelids taut
Before aroma permeates the air like incense
This is how to extend that Corona commercial
With those shallow marks we call actors
Evan Longoria looked great happily clad in
G2, in legato

Semi attached to a red-head,
But not Mir and a Herr
Who burns on the pages and orange cover
Makes you want to try something
Bolder than bold and fresh
And I just thought we were floating
Effortlessly in our own comforting sphere
I could call hearth, back in 74',
Briefly before you perfected coitus on legions,
Tricked by every shimmering tide
Again and again
Thrown haplessly like a spinner
Flapping thru water's shadows
I get the gist of life now
Do you know who you are
A farmers daughter
Or just another belching wren

"Swagger"

Loss claws at my innards
The way crows reenact prancing to
The throes of death, decay so
Feverishly
As if their lone entities scathing
Against a callous world
That falters to demands
People like me or like you
Even cheats with the name (Starr)
To raise ourselves from wounds
Some ballooning of crooked bowed misses
You could call fate of our signs
But whew, born again from ashes;
I don't know
And a line in a path Blaine crossed
Burned hollow
As my soul becomes divided from
Importance I swagger to
The simple worship I had of you, was dreamy passion
Worse than the pain beauty extols
So ravishingly
When it leaves or comes knocking
Putting minds in a fog
Too hard to obviate her
Pretentiousness

Stepping back like a bird
Wadding for her on this corner
Like a prancing rockette
Until all this vulpine talk ends
Marked by change and a smile
Until she says, "Let's go."
As were creeping to some kind of
Mortality seldom seen
The sky is pinned gray over hemlocks in
Manhattan but nobody cares

"Reflection"

Could've we painted a portrait in precession
The kind heads smile and crane at
To in this life
Would've it been real for long
Or just another lie and coaxing
To someone I strongly believe
Is more than hydrogen thought
Pouring down from the heart
To the feet,
As my reflection wanes
But you could've acted on every
Innuendo
Are you really so self-satisfied?
Two drawing on this composite,
Ethereal at a Twain companion
Hinder is a world only dreamed of
All that can't be mended only imagination
Drowns in your limbs, baby
What happened to all the standards
Of a lost craft, all that exudation
These things we talk about called
Potential
A dangerous place to cross that ebb
Watching over us
Two kids etched on acidic paper
Seeing things as they humanly are
Is a lonely reflection

"For effect"

I pulled the cap off a frozen Harp bottle
Watched frozen hops before they stirred to the knurled lip fizzed,
Agitated by the light of a fake stained glass light or oxygen
Behind it's glass heat like an obscure lens dark like walnuts
The beer looked like a frozen glacier in a snow globe, a jag
Melting slowly uncapping
One lump like snow hitting my throat almost chokingly
Another in about 7-seconds, something Patrick would've
    extolled
Then a complete rewarding beer Bud knows little about
Now Shock-Tap that Michelob
Over golden fries and a Blue Moon
Then we crossed hairs, lip before flirting with disaster casually
Adorned by sashaying hips so passionately affecting
And side-bars with Katey and Dani about nothing as if we had
    paresis
Bartenders I wish were nieces
True messengers of healing psychiatry so inculpable
Laughing at our distinction and the trick beer

"Bundled joy"

Bundled joy
Won't keep you in the end
Whilst most humans don't matter
Till you find someone who cares without rascality
And then that becomes lost
Shuffled like those Morgan dollars we used for grocery shopping
In the 60's
The message that I send hopefully not a sad note forgotten
Girl friends followed him, souls bared pitifully
To find their own darn luck or be lastly inept which is it
All that you thought you cannot lose, left behind
Trimmed from sight
A trait of living to accumulate is exhausting
One thing just a placebo for another
Stuck in the middle no longer finding appeasement
Or little formula
What's worse than living a life so full
Is not having the expectation
I had of you more than balanced risk
Locked inside the confines of the mind
Where a heart exfoliates like deaden leaves
Or ripped silk like exhaust frees in a whisk

"So tenacious"

I watched one pre-teen, so tenacious
Happily teeter on a yard's black swing
Affixed to the approaching intersection
I turned my car onto
Her eyes also affixed to a caring sky
Nearing the cask of dawn
As if she could tabulate her bold future
No one could waver, even a boy wearing musk
Soon to know how things change in a blink
But I'm not calculating stock's worth
The water snake inhaling the water strider
Across from Ringing Rock
And the plans you thought you made as you watch the coffee
    maker distill
There isn't much to filter thru at 50
The true journey begins
With the small steps of a child,
But when I schlep into that room
As much as I've been scorned
I couldn't ditch the desire
Weaving a patch just to get to you

"Gold dust woman"

Leslie,
Use to ride horses with obnoxious names
As if they were suggestively flirting us
With her time surely not a clown princess
Singularly obverse to all competition
One's name was "Da Ditto";
"Can't Hide Me"; and "Standing Alone"
Sometimes at the finish line winning
Deserters laying backward
You stood once standing on your toes
Stretching on the glimpse of a backstretch's loam
Talking to us
Probably felt like breaking down
Coming off any mount
With Mt. Zion courage
Takes recovery time
You had a gold or silver tooth shining
I saw conversing, wedged against the fence
I remember something you said before retiring to
Florida
"I'll ride for you." Exclaiming your pride I guess
And then about 9 yrs later
You had an entry at Tampa;
But I forgot her name, until now
Was the initials of a former girl-friend
JR's Exchange

"Pointing to"

I see
All these early indications
My wisp sounding grandson
Like a willow waving
He needs little motivation
To pull his filled tugboat thru
Life
Using a fierce, bravado, determination
To get my full attention
He uses his sunny smile
It's not fair for a boy to have all that charisma
It's a sparkling shimmer
Even in a late evening, he say's
"Come on take my hand, let's play
Upstairs."
With two lightly inflated plastic balls
One pink and one blue
Resembling a soft-ball without seems
The ones that have a nipple
Where you blow air into
Then I retrieve the balls
Bouncing off the ceiling in a planned skirmish
Gyrating like an exotic dancer, that I'm not
I feel as if I'm his safety decoy
Rubbing me to arouse his senses
And then he becomes typically bored
Like adults
And distracts me with marbles
That are translucent
Extraordinarily he rubs
The Jeanie in the bottle
Towed to the turpitude of growing
He doesn't mind
Soon he'll be rifely found

"One for dawn"

My favorite time
Except when having bad dirty dreams
As if reaching for silk fibers that aren't there
Is when dawn pokes forward
This quietude I'm so accustomed to
Living with untamed lethargic shrews
Before a day's usual tumult
The thoughts I had running momentarily
Like Kerouac's type
Is all I kept and a breeze along my forearms
Hands tucked under your skirt in Feb.
Turns off all this negativity I feel
And that exuding smile that kills
Even a model's grief almost makes me keel

For Anita

"Lost again"

Real closure
Begins after the growing years
I know (two) guys who could corroborate
A spin doctor's thesis
Or their own when forgotten
Worse than being alone on a side-walk
During a fierce cloud burst
Forgotten by all
And quirky nature wrestling to forewarn
Please include me
You may see at the bottom of a pool's
Still, olive glassy cover
A soul approaching foreclosure
Even when "believing" is so hypocritical
Many dismal tomorrows I awake to,
But Sara said, "I'll see you again,"
Why, and 'AJA' eyed me with admiration and
Caution
All the time I didn't get her number yet
Afraid she'd respond
I didn't want to tether on more eventual loss
But I won't be forgotten
Even if I try again

Born on a new chance
Never fearing one measure of decry
All the things we rummage to running
Like Zimmy on trains
Moving continental to unfamiliar liking
So accustomed to all that's naïve
As if you were a cluster of seeds becoming nascent
On a waft
Obsessed by the complimentary wiggery passenger
The feigning nymph of forestry
Gallantly pressed to a challenge
Lost again, but not in turmoil
As every avenging heart looks to the gutter
But who can foil all this christening
Before eating the hearth bread

"Filling in"

Filled hearts
Like were ground particles
In our own underground play
Love so gratis
But ones vacant as untapped wells
A majority of the lonely unhinged
Where passion hides deeper
Uninhabited as sea scrolls
Where ebullience can't be seen
Or spoken about except in every eclipsing
Eulogy so plural
Is this how the empty hearts
Spend their time? Writing uninhibited
Slighted by companionship
Trying to feel estimable
Is everything really for naught
The way Chabon describes
Living as not really neighborly
Living beneath the lines or borders
As everything becomes nebulous
When in youth's splendor, "Cindy"
Were we in some kind of phantasm
Trusting bodies in co-op, trading rides
Convoys and beautiful distractions
Now all this emptiness, to-dos

Makes me deal in contrivance
And then divagate tirelessly
When there's a female involved
Are you, I just postulating
To the demon
To find ourselves
On night-times dew
Just to destigmatize
Souls
Back to dexterity
And the Deer Park run-off
Clear as a mountain spring
Stalls to progression
And then gushes on top of your belly
I was wondering what you instill
Under those dangling hemlocks

"These names"

When I had time
Slowed to feel the daily atmosphere
Changing
Wow like birds with binocs'
Am I closer to Waldon's Pond
Viewing a lake in Sanatoga?
Thinking like Garrison Heillor;
Forgetting even to call Bill
About our slumping Phils
Slowly making their move back up
Sorta like Frank Wright always did
Sweeping adversity away
And the awe of that waterfall
Must be hypnotizing near Ohio
And damn that Yeats'
For not living until I was born
All these names just as great
A timeless catch
That Callison made

"Baring a soul"

Getting my own way
Has it's repercussions, sharing a life
Doesn't have to
Upset the balance of most compromise
Men know little about and some women too
But it seemed okay to have another drink
And come home late
Even Bree Olsen said it's almost impossible
To have just one soul mate
That makes sense, but I'm not a porn starlet
With budding features whose structured
I live in half-a double Victorian
To me that seems too communal
Leaves me dazed and confused
It screams to me, come on change the décor
As in tasking would make one therapeutic
Sometimes I need to shuffle the balance
To find am use who speaks softly
But then I hear a voice that says,
"You should've called, and told me something."
Now I don't know who I was with anymore
Because the patches of silvery moon
Crest we gloss over so temporary,
Hypnotically to morning light
With an abandonment that can fracture
Purpose
Some may ring on redemption
I'm still begging for some recognition
As if I'm a hidden ore

"Wavering"

Trees and their waving leaves
Nature's post with unknown messages
Filtered to nutrients
From the sun's bursting power
But stars seldom crash and burn
Vertically on our g-force
Mine waits dimming
Exhaustingly
Flicker lower
Until you came germinating my cells
I've forgotten the fun we had
All that Zaniness
Made me glad to know you
Is to tout
Every accomplishment
And these overbearing obstacles
We create ourselves
Painting landscapes to starving artists
Never towed to denials

"Before relenting"

Could've I lost everything I had
Even favorite bartenders
Move from place to place
Simply lef the soft pretzels
In Dad's fridge for moisture
And the hearing aid on the marble table
Faceless to all as a fading sun like clams
Hiding under water's base
As gem beauties walk on the purest sand
In Temporary exiles called luxury
Mindsets clenched to portfolios
Held myself fastened to withering youth,
Again and again as if against a force truly
Turned to Eve my martyr and muse
More I had to lose in our new millennium
To a slow emasculation at forty-four
Held you like 45-karats without so much
Immense words as condoler connects
With a trusting comraderie;
And a kiss as soft as a light billowing wave
Carrying sucrose
Knowing we all can't be sui-generis
So we succumb to an even axes I can't be part of

"Recast"

I was torn
Between what is and not, trying to be recast
As Thoreau would've said more gracefully
Sweeping to the intellectual masses
You tried to be so mindless and still so tidy
As the grasses we watched ethereally
Sometimes as sheared as Wrigley in July
I wanted to see you again; why does this hurt?
But no one would take me there
Back-stage just to look in those emerald eyes
Swearing to get back a little time
So I was perched in row (M) – fifteen,
Finally after two and a half-hrs
All the crazed fans departed
And then I was met by you, you said,
"Please move quickly forward."
We looked like two disgruntled blue jays
On a lawn in the past
And you had the sheen of a marveled raconteur
As if you mockingly were playing on recrudescence
Love's silence shouting in the air as you smiled
And you were still slightly zonked on uppers

"You could've called"

You could've called, before summer
After the blinking bird's eye
That opening shutter of dawn
Mary
It bustles and watches over us
Would I postulate to be so true?
Need to hear an officious voice
Even more than seasonally
Would I unknowingly be attractively
Perverse
Needing a friend to talk to
To burnish so little that is,
Pleasant
As feathers laying in thick uncut grass
Warped again by time's translucency
As we transgress to nothing
But subtle changes
Like on postage stamps
Waiting for Katherine the Great's
picture

"This Love"

I now know what unconditional is,
This truculent love
The love you give to each of them
So excitedly sublime
Lost ours like exhausting
Subjugated ruins at large
And the smell of dying ethanol
Dropping
Evaporating on grounded leaves
Love like a submitting carcass
A pig gallant in death
To be roasted on even coals
But the soul lastly freed
From flatbed storage
Happily lost on the troposphere
Beats it's wing where lips engage
Without the plague of nicotine

"Turning to"

Sometimes I feel as anxious
As a summer squall, turning
As if someone is spurring
And then the inexplicable calm
When a sea or ocean looks chalky and/or
Clear as mercury
We as people become inflectional
As bending light, but the sight of God
Infiltrating fear
Is not easily understood
Was I exhiluting my own self control
At a time of infirmity
It seems now so hallucinatory
Under a sheepish quarter moon
A naked angel bending
Against the car hood
Moving like a shutter
With shimmering white skin
The passage of Jame's novel
That reiterates steady passion
Others aren't grateful for-
Like the thong-print on Nina
That invisible weave slight rank
To a ramshackle mind
Turning that door's handle
Is all that Ayn Rand could stoke
In an imaginary scroll
We'd have to speculate her interpretation
And someone's gold rush to gold rush
Ambition

"I couldn't help noticing"

I couldn't help wondering
About inanimate objects
As I was driving
Their power having a significance
The calmness of nature dubbing pain
Maybe better than real faltering
Contact or sexual tension
We thrive to reinvent constantly
I had passed an ancient willow on Rt. 663
It's branched leaves hanging,
Sloped like pointed arrows over lime
Chains
Reminded me of this life in bondage
Only freed by these images of nature
That never seem sepulchral
But the decay of raunchy composts
Breeding new life to plants
I've heard people say, "throwin the
Fish" the ground is eager for food
But still I couldn't help noticing
Of that vast reservoir along Pennsburg's
Borders with it's big mouth and shade
Waiting to be inhaluted
Griping as my tries inch away
To the real greed of humans
Each with a careful plan
That nature can denounce
Quickly as Hollywood reinvents Katrina's
Aftermath
From what I saw

Someone who wanted to paint
The first hours of evening
The way fireflies shimmer
The night explicably
Even for those on the underground
Require the humanity of strangers
Dully in hidden café's
You blew into my cold hands
Repeated the gesture
And then laughed at the curious
Existentialist in me

"Feign to"

The closest I've got to probative prostitution
Was being a night laborer for a profiteer $
Or talking to porn stars
With names like Kendra, Victoria, Trixy,
Alicia and Francesca Le, really her name
Drawn to these sketchy profiles
Maybe collage didn't work out
What a service Hartley performed acrobatically
They seemed so profusely down to earth in person
Instead of gutters that don't resist
It's as if they could shrug anything in their way
My passenger, friend said there goes one
Crossing a vacant street passing the lone tattoo shop
At Franklin and High
She had on a tight leather jacket and jeans
Was she waiting to pass her sweets
Just out of the pen
Or searching for Phenobarbitals

"To the invective"

I have neighbor's
Who act like I'll rub off on them
A venomous spew
So filled with hate
I can't excuse them
Think their divinely above
Any power of God or suffragen
Want me to stumble or lie down
Since I was raised to love all;
You don't matter, either
You can't crucify me while I'm alive
I can't be really frowned upon
Cover my casket with firm dirt and flies
I'll push all your hurt aside
We do live in a time frame so filled
With divide
You better revise where you think your
Going to could be a place so snarly
God macerates all evil
And glorifies the poor
That might be something that knows you

"The wait"

Every dream broken as fodder
As if I'm waiting for the big crunch
Lay crushed like a Molotov bottle
Smoking to gray
Now cold as the eloping La Nina
And what follows so blurring mad
Samantha awaits in the fancy boudoir
Where Hollywood greats hang subtle
(you) before spinning woofers howl in
Succession
No need to feel so slumber
Casually bumbling into my crush
Slender as the Virginia slim ad of yore
Winking and flashing cell digits
As her eyes sleuth the masses
Of flotsam minds buoyed to indifference
Slier is exuding desperation
So glad you could come

"Wildly" (Intoxicating)

Tackling on
How one cultural (icon) may've felt
Dazed to others conformity
Admirably when becoming their cytoplasm
Must've been endearing
On that "Owl Farm"
To learn early on
How cut off from society is kind of
Hardening guest
Getting by on your own margins
Now it seems a tuft on elbows or seems
To everyone influential or truthfully
Controversial as we all are
Attuned to his own beliefs,
Never silenced
Continued as the vein of (Twain's)
Whoop verse
Someone so solid to his friends
With a weird afterglow, in passing
He still can wince away all pain
When I think of him,
Stoking fear with wild rushes

"Remembrance"

My brother use to hide bits of stew
Behind a radio on our kitchen table
Our neighbor "Chut" did drugs
And then set his house on fire,
He also use to eat all the Prince's stickies
My dad use to use Morgan Silver dollars
For spending money on groceries
How gross losing 0.7734-per oz.
I use to wait on the corner of
Mt. Vernon with Denise and the deviant
Barb for a bus
To take us to Patts town High
Those sputtering sounds nearing
From exhausts so lonely
Knowing it was rounding the corner
With it's fixated color of Oranage
Stopped and nabbed us defiantly
As if we were criminals it seemed
But slowly what a crescendo
When we left
And all I remember are some home-
Room curves
And peek-a-boo lips that looked like
They could croon over...

"This passion"

Feel like the world's crash dummy
The ones you don't see in commercial highlights
That fail
Would be bad for any business
Sometimes to be as fickle as a thermometer in
Winter
Don't have a reason to be so fidget
When all have let me down
Just like a caving sea wall
Behind those light houses
But I can't wear a frown
When tomorrow breaks enthralled to Bridget
Supported to what was right, and
All that was wrong
I'm glad I don't have a young fiancé
Could never be that strong to trust in infinite stars
That beg for renewal crashing
But I will burn to you this epiphany
Of all that's merry and festive when were together
I might also be netted and knurled
To all of hell's throng
Don't miss the feverish run to a wrong journey
Before I'm beset by rolling thunder
You made the jocose proposition
Standing naked in briefs
Perverse to the hail of moonlight

A glistening glare
To the whitest toned thighs
And a multitude of leaves that
Listen
We'll have more fun than Pluto
When the multiplex closes
I got a key and I hid the
Jameson on ice
Come back at a quarter unto two
I'm sure we can find something
To do or reset a movie

"Where I was going"

Sometimes I feel
I have failed myself the most
Barked up the wrong tree I was going to
Let's make a toast to wrong doing
I didn't even scrape any white birch on my skin
Falling down
And I could never escape every changing moon
Alters the gears in me
And then they become undone and straggled
I told someone it was God's plan, soon
Now how could I ever like just one
When love is tucked in every corner
Dangerously
Even the man behind the pulpit
May need an existing subpoena
Just to be free
Love is found on the subliminal trajectories
Just as easy in haunts
At which we sit gregariously numb
This heated trance so hard to diffuse
Just hoping it don't make the mind transgress further
Wasn't I, you brought here to entertain a fine lady
As if it was my duty
With my hand on my chin with little equanimity
For sure
She saw thru all this chagrin and fear
Like a kinsman
And I said emphatically with a few words so clear

"Brush up with some Maybelline,
And meet me near the rear door
That entrance that ends like a cul-de-sac."
I don't need no plan to escort you
As you heart swoops on mine
God leniently hangs beside me
In every calm Atlantic storm
My liaison and me walked through with quite levity
Into the arms of a night that won't pass
I still wonder about each lass
Like the loyal passerine
Somewhere a peacock that can't be pegged
Roars in the valley of d....
Where I was going

"Patchy"

Who could I pattern myself after?
Is that hwy I search for antique quilts?
To find a "worded" stitch
Taking me far away maybe Paine
Could've sniffed benign once
I don't know anyone who hates all
Liberalization
Ferret to the name Bortner
And an ancestry so foreign
Lost from coast to coast
A few relatives buoyed somewhere
I could be like Kennedy
Who cared for all races and
Our waning sovereignty
Or I could be like myself lost today
Shuffled as the policies of OBama's slant
Can no longer govern effectively
Without the usual predicament
To loss the happy ticket
By not changing congress
And being tough on bad laws
Goldberg sees as an atrocity
I just can't be someone else's
Prodigy
So I'll try to be higher than hope
But just what is the desideratum
To be like Jack Kerouac
Steadily patchy I guess and
Intertwined

"What you take away"

I let you take away the plush sawdust
Seeds of my dreams
That Candace B. penned
My eyes couldn't watch feebly
Turning manhood
Into the burnt film of coal
To not lay beneath someone
Close to their inner most makings
To feel their scent like rushing salt water's
Stain
And the oneness of curves lost
Is the iniquity of a slow death
You cause
But I still find buoyancy
As you furrow closer
To your own damnation, alone
Lubricious to the touch
I am forever scorned as the venom rises
I saw...

"Imbrue"

Oh, how time washes (us) away
All sincere thoughts
As a heart tires of waiting
Hopelessly
Could I be in an Russian bread lines
Because of totalitarianism
I dreamed of many
But you can't begrudgingly
Trudge those listless, dull stairs
To do your duty
I call the Bijou pact
Is it so trashy lacking panache
Or are you just so impalpable,
Why should I care?
There is some unknown immediacy somewhere
That I haven't imagined
Beyond the placard and tape
Measure

"The stain of singular vision"

When each day was so bitter and long
Like sea birds who can't find food
Along a water's shelf by dusk
Right then, I needed you to make me
Feel
More lively and different again
When one self thinks their below
Reproach
Is this a sense of betrayal so common
If it happens more than once
Rolling over all that's conventional
Is this just the dutiful and gravity
Swoop
Of God's plan
Were so oblivious to

"Potentiality" (rests)

I can't live up
To what they want me to be,
Should i
To fail on others terms not mine
Before drowning
I already leased my life to others
And all this roughage shows a frown
I submerge to these dry concrete barriers
Conflicting walls that can't speak
Pass one word of silence before I weep
If I let you win just once again
To subjugate your tender beauty
Is a glove sweet temptress
And then to feel this cryptic guilt
Why is it as if I'm scrounging to a doused
Flame
That looks like amber lips half-enclosed
And after all the abandonment,
The one you chose to cull
And then dress up falsehoods to is gone
You can never quite replenish yesterday
And make it pacific again
Now I can try again without you
I'll make a mental list
And I'll never know if your as true
As the linen you wear
Glad you stayed the little girl
It seems I'm related to in another life
When you spoke it was as if I were choking for love

"Growing aura"

That young face
That once inspired
Even her elders, burning
Now breaking, clutching
Some coerced denial
Relentless the talk of coffee house papers
As if they willed you to be anchored down
Now course as gravel
Your pain now subsiding a bit
To clear the rush toward addiction
Thinking it would all go away
As my mind dwells
Just to say hello Jersey girl
Absorbed by your light aura
And those imbue freckles on your face so impartial to others
That wear the changing seasons
You only had to ask for friendship
I've caught on to you for years

For Lindsay

Del Louis

"Middle age"

What a battle to find the truth
Inside my caustic brain
As if two charred lost hands are drudging
Hard inside tall cylinders
Slavishly to wake me in cold Duluth
And every thing becomes cheesy as
If were cuckoos dallying to Wisconsin
What a deed thinking ones lost all?
Me and a friend still so discombobulated
Taller to not be on a quest
Quieter to let things become debased
And the queen will come in character
With arched eyebrows like a wave
Where we stood next to a stained counter
Our brains punching in thoughtlessness
Again because Metallica said,
"Nothing Matters"
So think fast anyway and ponder a
Plan
Before you miss the gristle of middle-age

"So unlikely"

Can we only see the future so unlikely
From our uncanny imaginations
Or the derisiveness of astrologers
To likely horoscopes
So sad to bear it alone it says were passive
Read a few good ones in the post
I saved for the (Cancer) sign
Didn't yet laminate the words boldly
I believe will someday ring true
So a child or a laggard finds them for wisdom
When he reaches that point so haggard
The maunder trail of those not loved
Better to spare their feelings
But not other things so sovereign
Greater those sea salt lips
The wind blows against
Convey God's calming nature
As gulls like floating clouds coo
Aren't we renders schmaltzy
Grandma can't get me to play
Scrabble ever
Laying the breastwork for play
Or living
With interjection like a pontiff
My niece exhibits all that's
Cool and prodigious
Even when picking lint off her

Paisley skirt
I hope she patterns something
From me
As if it were a secret code
Our mute manners
That reach our souls
Some things become apparent
From these horoscopes
At least a partial rendition
Of who we are

"So altered"

I think because I'm younger than him
He hates me my father
Is it because he can't think past
All the mistakes along the perilous way
The some one's I've made without change
All these broken straws
The path of family altered
Remember Trixy diversely
Standing naked in a fur coat at John's door
A dangerous beauty so pixy
Changing all that I critique and mentioned above
Because it was too painful even hearing the last
Echo

"Inspiring"

I had to leave
Where I was smothering
To go back to a founding decree
Inspired to what I believe is (True)
Wasn't all this denial
Eased from this waning flare, hope, pain
The fear of tomorrow chased down
By the unrelenting sun breaking
Earthly beholden to little
And be embolden
To one smiling stranger
Angela selling coffee's with those
Empirical looks
I never thought I'd have
And still have the empathy of another
That doesn't ever quite leave
Like the white gulls of a vivacious spring once
Back again
Emblazon on the macadam of strip malls, beside Weis's Market
Eager for my wonder bread

"Balanced"

To not evolve
Is to not find exultation
Even in her balanced eyes
Steady factoring in
As lips slightly curl to a drink
Lubriciously
As if they whisper
While breathing like air condition
Breezes thru
Many just the factotum
Of multi-tasks
Wisely, unconsciously nearing all this
Potential
We could call mediocrity
Wasted being a caregiver with honor
You sit there looking pomp and
Succulent
As if you could quell a sea
One vignette splendidly slant to all things
As Ava or Kate of Hollywood yore
For there is little facsimile
And beauty is scorned

"Scaring me"

Breakdown the barriers
Brace yourself to compromise
Lose your will
For more dissolution comes
Cementing little cure for toilet seat love
Do you ever envision
This scary insufferable act
You thought only others did
Of desperate interlaced people
Sometimes I even embrace the kindness
Of chunky Hispanics at (1402) when its 2 a.m.
This strike against beautiful people
When there is no cure, but massage parlors
For toilet seat love
It has that craned look so needy
Some porn grannies
Look devilishly better bobbing
With no denunciation at 65 or 47
Hartley's voice inside my head,
Says "Don't do her"
If she loses weight
It will intensify the act or is it too late bouncing off rubber
Choosing to defer every preference
As our delicate nature reflects
All that's savoir fair in mocking

"The last time"

You must've known, but I didn't ask
You, what I meant
When your cemented to another obviously
Does your heart pound like thunder
As you froze the last time we met, why
I've often wondered what we would've
Been like,
Even under satin sheets together
Vested like two birds weathering all
Opposition or change
In the loneliness of more lean years
But now your gone somewhere
Exceeded every time frame without
Risk of any kind
And I still feel the same way

For Tara

Del Louis

"Nearing all of us"

Jack was
And still is the desire and
Broken dream
Of all man
And their fading billow
Those blue eyes fanning girls
One's never denied
Something so binary
Until death's calming darkness
Lay those pipe dreams
And soft crescent feathers
To all who knew
This charismatic French American
Now starving to hear him
On any page
To placate our own madness
With his rolling, pivotal joy
Someone might ask or say,
"That was God's son."

"Humpty dumpties"

Humpty traipsing in a longitude line
Sweeping like a strong wind
Over gray dull crags some cut like zagged panthers
Along the Pacific Coast Highway and no. (10)
Waiting for the world to save their dumpster lives
Like crows in despair over flimsy roughage or lost innards
Humpty scraping my soul in excess like a temptress
As I painstakingly move on
Humpty looking for lard to a fire, anyone's
Brought down by his/her defying manner was a ploy
Crushing the grooves of discipline
Falling to a pit so unsavory
Not the holes on road no. (5)
And still I caught you
Filled every resounding fear

"This will of mine"

Do you have a will like mine
Met to the world's differences, the hidden flaws
And their crossbow marks
Weren't there signs after birth
The soul soon followed nature's callous fall
Or associations to all bad luck
As if I were a hypochondriac, but I'm not
It's hard to see a hybrid tomorrow
When all that was fiery and hip
Turns ashen
Not even a little cover
Waiting for your presence
And all that it holds
Is a ghostly imitation
Of all I imagine

"Surrender to"

Dear God-
Speed something solid to me
Heated like benzene
And the suns a minion streaking for miles
Like Lance in the Tour de France
What a license to style
Send your beauty
Thru my sweating pores
One whose fable is true
Saw all the lonely answers
In the white lilies
Shaped like Gina's lips
Here on this short patch of lawn
Suddenly I was light-hearted
Even feeling all the cosmos
You can see in Van Nays
Despite all of these counter attacks
Fried from all that I lack
Can you help me again
I feel like the small orphan
Whose spirit sweeps a rural cottage
And then disappears
Was I ever mentioned by you
Something said so resounding

Don't care to be declined by the masses
So I don't have to feel this dread
And all those ashen glares mean
Nothing
God, please help me be bold
I'm at your luminous threshold
To your surrender
And I saw you open a hand
With my eyes
Like a lighted lamp
With the smell of sulfur
So similar to sea salt
Grazing the cheeks and air
Another further approach to
Understanding you

"Too tired"

Oh how I dread this life
And don't know
Anyone who wants to be cared
For
I'm so tied to a cold rusty
Nail
Need a neat fifty for the
Gambling parlor
To make Robin happy with a quire
Score
So damn tired of all the debt
I've inherited it makes me so
Squalor
Now we've got a president
Who is against reform
Trying to steer a train wreck
Of a deficit
This isn't what lawyers are
Trained for
Good luck brother soon you will
Feel
The spurn
I've felt a long-time ago
To swear is abiding
Someday I'll get it right
Not become the object of a

Policeman's spotlight
Funny how prestige and
Everything fades
Into a basin or the sea
They say LA's sewage
Is cleaner than it's gutters
And I'm too tired to utter
The epitaph of what capitalism
Means
Shown in every bell graph
It's meaner than an angry boar
In Arkansas
Maybe things will change
Today
We were meant to be something
Time or folks can't disclose
We were meant to sway in the
Shadows
Down here by the bay where
No one's forsaken

"Without a plan"

Dawn
Giving me
The contingency
Of tomorrow's path
Without foregone conclusions
I know little about
Adjoined to my obeying circuitry
And pumped blood
Under a chrysanthemum sun
Breaking like a fast ball
As if your own christening
Was thoughtless as swept wind
Only the lonely hear
That pitter-patter of feet or rain
Nature's angry passerby
Then dusk' comes so unstressed
With it's quilted moon
Must be the pipe dream
Of failed responses,
Can't anyone dial me
The carelessness of others
I to am partial to
And marginally inept
Still like the night's streakiness

We could've been bound to
Before darkness fosters
Another sweep
To flickering equality
Or sexual fervor born
By mindless play
Of a past drove away
To joyless barren prairies
Now adjoined to the flea bane
Knowing the contortion
Of butterflies diagonally flitting
In meadows with patterns so consistent
As if I were one of Jack's beats

"Fatherly"

Grandfathers
The forgotten part
Of a families undertone
All of varying degrees of man-hood
Some fatigue from being
Fatherly
Their grandchildren
Fixing mores constantly changing
A rainbow's unification
A raw staple they carry o'
Unto life
Grandfathers still
Needing them as tutors
And provoking rules
Under their own obey
Like squirrels under maple
I try to stem their flow of
Defiance with lecture
Show them how to progress
But let them learn
We to are driven by errors
These failure's that make us
Begin again
To reach the stamen on a limb

"Without a plot"

Tonight
This Irish haunt seems somewhat anew
When you skirted thru this place
In your evening attire
My soul began burning again
Were you meeting someone, do you need someone
To talk to
I haven't seen a face like that
Or eyes so aglow
In a long time,
And I just said, "What do you wanna do."
Theresa,
And then she said, "Let's stay here a little longer,
Just tempt our drinks
Before we take a walk
Past those rigid railway spikes that protrude
Into an awakening darkness filled with fireflies
That spit the sweetest tune."
But now I'm immune to your power
And I'm not laying in this grass helpless to be just what you want
While many sleep under dampened cardboard
And those trusses
What a blessing to see you

"Disconnect"

Lately
The 2nd immediate family
The one I've inherited thru marriage
Has gone array
Someone or me has become so bungled
How could something so pure
Become denigrated when it had a worthy
Intentional plan
Are they, this the usual disconnect
Is this the path of Lucifer;
I cannot be behold to his confusion
Is nothing more than deception
My chaos is adjoined to the living, eventually
All bad weather turns clouds
Righteous blue and stern sooner or later
And if things don't turn out eventually even
I won't be rightfully remembered
Like kids at play in childhood, lastly
Cemented in someone's memory
Is the book with un worded portraits
Of others dreams so foreign to one

"Dark Beauty"

Penelope,
Your beauty
The death grip of longing
So unparalleled
You could perpetuate riots
And when you talk in repartee
It's as if you've broken grammar and T's
Casually
Unfold like the sweetest dark
Plum
Teases before it leaves a stem
And those lips the perfect
Suffice
As if your kiss was remitting
Sin

"Patch"

I may be
Completely out of sorts
As worn as you patch on makeup
Did you see thru me
I might just need
The wisdom of a blind woman or
Man
But I can't understand why
I'm lonelier than a patch of dirt
The kind dogs sit alone next to
Without the seed of a blossom seen for
Yards
Your like a soft patch
On an old pair of jeans
And I don't know what's in the cards
Left sitting rumbled
But when you talk
I can feel something comforting
To both of us
Is that just a conundrum
And I was thinking
You might be good for me
I'll even let you
Turn the plead in the cover first
I don't know if we should go any
Further
My eyes on you is enough
Like all the cattle I've seen
Bracingly odd to tomorrow's trust
Hitherto
Stay still or meet me at the end of the
Line

"Teller"

Laura
Works at the bank tenaciously
One who I can hardly relate to
Past forms and money
I call her Isla Fischer
Somehow, I'd like to get to know
Her a little
Life is so temporal
More so now
That she lifted her sweater
With a move so provocative
To reveal a tattoo over that velvet skin
Down the small of her back
All I ever get
Tidbits of the real thing
Behind tektite
[unreadable]
Past a shield and counter
Where all is hidden

"Everyday"

The mundane things in life
Aren't just for the artist's gain
Brushing his thoughts
They are for the less articulate
Even the low growth deposits of
Sagebrush
Never for naught on the rock
George Washington stood on
Most people treat religion
With skepticism or as gainfully
Mystical
Or as a condition that could cause the
Mumps
How could I going to Sunday school
On a corner at High St.
Set there on purpose with masterly
Intentions
All those mundane things
We practice unconsciously
Our daily boring routines
Though some aren't meant for tradition
They get by below the margins
Where society snares us without a
Treatise
And how about mammals and all that
Aquatic life in zoos

Waiting for the zigzagging customers
As if they were darting neon tetras
For what, to pleasure us and then profit a few
An elephant with a proboscis has more sense
Than law makers who willfully still pass
Property taxes when half the nation is unemployed
Or on fixed incomes
Making us so torpor to get back
And then I have a friend who acts so profuse
Only with his tongue and words
Not actually accountable to others everyday
I guess probably the things that aren't mundane
We remember the most

"Now, tell me"

If I'd ask you
How you look so gracefully
Good
In those closing years of middle-age
If you told me something of
Pertinence
Would I then coyly know my place,
Would you half mockingly say,
"By having a good man,"
Or thru a half sentence also say,
"Why do you ask."
Maybe I just wanted to touch
A heart
And see if it's beautifully speckled
Whilst in desperation mode,
Hasten like the migratory grafter I'm not
Expecting green house effects
In bursting converse
Until you smiled like a man
On his briar
And the harrumph sounds clear
Now knowing I have your trust
Lusting for companionship
May seem a little unhallowed
But you eyed the same purpose
In broken English
Now, please tell me
What I'm after

"Fate"

Fate it surrounds me
Walks in circles like the unduly teacher
We choose to forget their name
Mrs. Bromberg use to cough next to my waist
It seems
I continually make the same silly mistakes
As if I slipped off a crag
Tossed into the deepest blue
Before I could make the decision to recover
I still pick all these names from nostalgia
And lost causes
Except in Street Cry
Pinched to a feeling you get out of construction
When someone playfully sits on your sternum
But if it's night time
There's not much else you can do
Unless you recover from fate by picking up a plastic
Sword

"These pictures"

I saw a tall black man
Walking on Glasgow with his girlfriend
Shocking to see his baby
Steadily moving behind him
In a little stroller
They were speechless with glee
As if they never had a problem
So picturesque seeing couples
In placid Hallmark strolls
His girl could've been named cinnamon
Close by, anonymous to this last trenchant world
With gluts shaped a heart pendant
Swaying from a chained necklace
Some of the things in this life
They just can't be explained
It just shows
Not everything in life has to be filled with
Stress
And then I leave my porch
By then everything's in disarray
Just as easy a splayed curtain leaves in a hint of
Sunshine
You tip toed and danced around

"Dating"

So tired of eating chuck
Maybe I'll get the mad-cow disease
As all luck moves sinuous
Ly in spurts like dating
Pick me up off my slumber
Anyone
With steak on my plate
To taste that gristle
On my lips
I have little rules for
Courting
Except of high-heels
And the surprise of thongs
Beside a few minor
Infractions
None towed to my mind
What's obscene is in the
Eye of the beholder
Many ways to marinate
The freshest chuck
Tastier than tough sirloin is
That needs to be pounded
Softer than your thighs at
Midnight
That frizz around my hands
Of sexual nature

"Kids of mine (whose complaining)"

I couldn't leave you
We've come too far
The worst "ordeal's" even a book title
Went past us
Just celestial waste
Dodging the scandium spread
Still sparkling but dimming
Could you set to see it on your rural porch
Now somewhere afar as Neptune
If I leave now there will be scars
I'd miss too much
London's yearning past trains
At least one graduation
Your girl-friends, Narissa
Juggernauts like Megan Fox,
So pretty
Your boyfriends I'd view as a scout
With skepticism
Think of me as your wisdom
In the backdrop corners of sacrifice
The twitching short-stop
That never evades you
Comes hell or high water crests
That dusty moth on abandoned garages
Beating
I'll protect you to
If danger should skulk you
For God-sake I'm yours grand-children

And more
I've seen you saddened by more than rain
These skirmishes are growing pains
Before adult-hood
Jay, testy as a wasp
I've seen you in (two's)
Happiest as can be
For it is sometimes always
Just like in love
I've nurtured you to be good
Don't intrude too much on God's
Way
He has a plan
Follow life's rules peacefully
Listen to the elderly
Help them in their despair
Remember we all get old too soon
Don't forget you were important
When I'm gone –
You'll be too busy to remember all
This or who I was
From a Schlemiel
Talk to me in silence
When your alone
Maybe in your mind
That room will be filled
With divine sparkle

As angels clasp on
They do indivisible, they do
In all my sorrows
You are the skylark over Germany
And my beated breast
Don't forget to care for London
Sometimes he gets the shaft
Free him from broken speech
Yesterday he was delighted by
Reflective light past dusk
Show him the way steadily
So I can rest without a grumble
And I'll feel the best whirl
Maybe I'll be
The swirl in your curtain
At morning's rush, souls start
On a vibrant path

"The last call"

We lose the last vestige
Of friendships
When we marry
Rights not granted to freely vent to
Someone
Then I called Cat
Because I was lonely
One dull summer
Couldn't break her
From the domesticity
Of her duties at home/cooking
But she must have felt
A shared sense of contiguity
Never one to be subservient when you're a
Scorpio
But with her anguished words and tone
She put me in my place, and said,
"You need affection I can't give you."
But I never said that before the last call

"Pining for the truth"

How can you stay in this union
Not shared by the traits of love
To be so disconsolate as I am lately
And you with nothing but contempt
That continually compresses
What is in your view-master
You can't possibly find meaning
Carrying on the way you do
I eaves-drop when you sit on the porch
Pining for the truth or some deity
Maybe just waiting for compliance
Without the usual compunction
Or the defoliation in Fall running for
Miles
Or something that pleases, I can't satisfy
Before easing my sorrows more
Or becoming somewhat blowzy
She blithely hung up this evening

"Never swaying" (before gravity)

These
Images the mind transport
Always frantic
Like lost love or freight spinning
Away
Do only fraudsters dream
Peering in their rum glasses
Sick of the daily lonesome fray
Never swaying
Easier to hate fourscore but I can't
In another 7... frame
As if were completely fraternal
Waiting to do idle things
That are fun in a transmutation
Tom-boy
T&T we could've been ignitable and
Stomping
Sliding down slick gables or
Walking hills that make desires
On fractal bends as a lens widens
It's now as if I'm the ibis darting
Down for little food
Furrowing down water in darkness
So deliberate
Like the lapsing horned toad
Melting into water like a drop of rain
Dissolving all traitorous thoughts
But one of you
Dark swan – for an Italian girl

"Measuring moods"

With every bright sunny morning
You'll be beating towards love and
Ambition
I'll be a gray cloud that passes you
Before departure's frown
If you can still remember me
As the thread that gave you
Dignity
Like any quilters
Though at times it can't be measured
When you become proficient
But captured by the world
When there's thunder on the mountain
And your not alone
I hope I lent you these miscible traits
Others adore
Don't mistake the tipping rain
Sweet as grog
Illuminating flashes
Thru air and limbs as a burden
It is a symbol you still have time
To embrace the oddly sustained mysteries of life
Passed me like deer darting at 90 – degrees
Pigeon holed to nothingness again
As we delve to their meaning
Might as well twist off a beer's
Bottle cap
So as to not imbibe rustic thoughts
And find the knurled nut crusher

To roast walnuts aglow on a fire
Knowing little we have an upper-hand on
But to defy the odds and streak
Or to be the safe mural on the wall
The one that seems to gallivant
Through a beaded sun
Smidgen at noon
As sugar spooned to hot coffee
Some would call a smudge
Embodying all that differential
In a world that's become mute

"Failings"

I'd rather be the man you can't have
Then be the one you want is stranger
The occasional illusion to posture freedom
Is not what we get or even posies
But it cuts thru this ineffable pain
As you waver from me unconditionally with a grudge
Having no choice but to be inebriated falsely
Or to freeze the failure of shared halves
Knowing I didn't mean to be insipid
It's a family trait
Now there's nothing left to stoke
Except the resounding muteness of honest

"This pain"

Pain can be forever
Or vague as subsiding sunsets that tear
Over a sanguine sketchy Halloween sky
Don't try to utilize it's meaning
Suffered as though
Poison doze was sprinkled
Over my heart
With you perverse chiding
Too late to enrage the sexes
Or these inflexible party leaders
Who hide beyond their fake charm
And white collars
Pain so unremitting to our physical world
Sometimes

"Among a poem"

You purposely
Destroy me psychologically
And then I pine before embarking
To be exempt before transmigration
From intrusion
And the everyday travails
Be bold and forceful before lapsing
Like bird's pecking for food
But smile at the opposition or oppressed
Dress up the day to challenge
The smallest desire still awaits you
As every sense tells you belong
Somewhere
It's opposite love so palmy
As scented laurel
So temporal
Leaves you in a minute's notice
Like spring
Know that every painkiller
Is the bartenders all etched in
Memory
Softly cooing that latent souls
That Charlie touches

"Brief encounter"

You in a fortuitous state
In your frilly underwear so sheer
Almost baring all
Sitting with white knuckles
Pressed against his bed
Two hearts so forsaken
One bearing a resemblance so challenging
Of all that was lost and forgotten
Just how much more can one man take
When the past has a reflector
She shined thru the moon's glance
Like an uncut jewel
Jaunty as the shadows playing,
Dancing juxtapose on the wall
Hiding any sort of incrimination
Shamelessly
Toiling thru excitement and
Modernization
As your moiré blouse moves like a
Wave
Ina short vignette

"These children"

You let these children
Foster flickering hope
Always burying your own
Signature care
When you need space
From this world without a thorough diarist
You can't face the beauty of middle age
Buoyed as their reflective anchor
Even if you want to rest
Beside a meadow in an old-fashioned hammock
Supping Mike's hard, you know
Or bundling twigs for art crafts
They are not getting to me
When you want to peel your skin
It's not that I'm too selfish
I wonder what they think deeper
Down in the wells of their spongy hearts
They must see a sad sea of darkness
Narissa, knows she must plough
Ahead to tomorrow Gladstone with a billowy smile
Sorrow leaves and then comes back
Like a dead knock against a wooden door
In a Eastwood movie
You let these special children ruin a lot

But what would they stake
Alone in a world bumptious
Without this trying love, and connect
This place could be a triangle
Of caustic fire or complete peace
Found in the company of strangers lastly
Pining for some truth
Can be a real awakening to kids
When loss is the essence of ascending
Past the furor of who we are
Know your individuality was a part of me
The tip of ancestry
Even if you become that recondite
Floating binary star necking below the heavens
And the remiss nebula
While the rest walk in their haze
Unable to negotiate life's turns

"Past 47"

The rawness of middle age testimony
Past 47
Only to leave a tinge to the young,
But Heather says, "I can go for
An older man."
She's so privy with conviction
We could be similarly nestled
On a rural path
Or I could feel the dead metastasis
Of a lizard's skin
Now regretting the nerve I once had
For subtle change
Is a river's flow
When on the cusp of a building crisis
I followed a crooked run road
Away from ancestry
Tired of all the mounting dilemma
Far from the contrast
Of Rembrandt's apples and oranges
But none the less eccentric and
Dutch
With Irish brooding blood
Calmed at the ugly oyster
Looking in Katie's eyes
Searching for the truth of middle-age
And what it was

"Past 47" (pt. 2)

The vision of middle age
So raw past 47
Then I felt comely sexual tension
Where you stood Nina in the Market
Suave as a milk shake
I froze like an icicle near a counter
All thought waning like a pauper in
Exile
I'll tell you later, why
I didn't say hello
Didn't want to break the chain of perfect
Company

"We could have fun"

We could have fun
Like squirrels that chamfer
With their hands
Count the ways we do it
As if Belladonna was cheering us on
Before turning sixty in (2017)
My father's time quite rough-shod
Even after Nixon and Vietnam
Was much different
Now we have technological gadgets
Called Blackberry's and lavish
Push button sex toys
But you'd rather brow-beat me
Into submission
I took temptation further
To ride the devil's oars
While our love was slitted
All traces unfounded
Fooled the same way
As men whose names carry on
Asterisks
Barry, who'd be the lasting judge
En route to Cooperstown
Or someone else's rapture

Irreconcilable differences
You with your iron curtain
Heart
But how could I loath
I wasn't brought up by those
Morals
I don't know with all the
Taking
Like a sickle to a field
Just what is it your staving
With your final need to be
Invidious as your daughter
I stayed piquant
Irreconcilable differences
The morph of their doom
I'd never let you see
How transcendental life really is
A cessation of labor
Met at a mind's cul-de-sac

"What's love"

Convince me
Even you lapping guidos before preemption
What's the biggest elusive quality to man?
Are you guys in a contraption to find love?
As you scurry for acception
Then the affection
It isn't found on a Forbe's list
Of monoliths of power
Maybe in a grocery store
It is found in the bracing of our differences
Speared to these emotions
Sometimes we need a contrivance
To get it, and then
To be ourselves before cooing
Sometimes it leaves us in a blink
This love that acted as a convoy harboring many
It escapes us at vacant door steps with no harmony
Except from these chimes dangling
Just what is it
That makes her love a ruthless entity man
And him a slovenly harlot on occasion
Maybe we want to be the saving harbinger
Accepting one-another for who we are (nay)
That takes someone rarer than any gem
We find in a window
And then you how tow on a sanded beach before dusk
Scented musk on your silk beside me smiling cutesy and curvy
As if God preceded to act and know this love

"Pointing"

So the lines have been drawn
Worn as a tethered opossum
Or single men trying to orchestrate the night's bow
Don's thoughts so bovine he was speechless to arouse
Attention to any older woman
Still in their golden age of ripeness
That time of great deliverance and a heart raging
When you can't crawl past your snout
Edging like a marsupial to the edge of the sea
Where ghosts in lighthouses stir and watch
Ships on fading motorists
And the flopping white broken mop's top of waves
As all thoughts clearly not in motion
Fade into gray skies and this darkness
Until your soft hands
Make a line across my lips
As you smile deeper down

"Enlightenment"

A more ancient form of life
Lived here or visited
More eccentric than the Dutch
Laid their tiny bodies
Near our sea beds
Would any action cam
Let us photograph them
With their bodies
With the silvery fish
To blend together like coffee
They studied us
Went back and forth
Toward space and earth
Closing in like binoculars searching
As aliens, didn't they discover hidden truths
Found on our planets
Of little worth
Except our nature so still, plumed
Now they watch baseball
Abhor news tabloid shows
And listen to "yes"
Oh, how the Air force
Suppressed the evidence
Of their being, at least Reagan knew
Something about a band of gypsies
Called the Raelians
I bet their wound tighter
Than knowledge
I wonder if they perform in an astral
Circus display
They probably can make themselves smaller
Hide in fluorescent bulbs

To recharge and watch us or plants grow
Decry and debunk our systems
The way the French do
Someday, maybe they will walk the earth
And concur
With more than corn stalks and crickets
That ricochet on side walks
Who wouldn't want to see if their hair is
Brittle as the teeth on combs
One said, "That guy Obama trying to thwart
All humanity on earth unless you're an illegal
Lest us take Courtney
She likes to burn dresses
And seems so different
Maybe we can program her
Those collagen lips went array
Maybe we can dicker her
To our program

"Shotty poem"

The tunnel vision of tomorrow
A velveteen vapor on trees 27 degrees
Replaced by the reality of today
With it's false varnish nature provides
Of what we expected was the truth
But the sun today
Almost burned your skin
Against the pendant
You wore in that cathedral
Stuck to your V-neck cashmere
As I am to you
More than an outward expression
That's estimable

"Acquaintance"

Lil
Called her Footloose
Tapped on my brain
Personable as sweet meat
And also a twin and masseuse in Oaks
I didn't get to know
Her sinewy frame
Dancing in thin air as if she's ethereal
Through non-descript aisles at Hollywood video
As if she were a sprite
In a fictional salacious play
Caught my noggin
With attentiveness talking about Broadway
And seeing 'Cats' ten-times
Between a Christmas card and a smoke for objectiveness
On the stoop
This curio took the non-stop to Florida
Exciting a life and boy-friend
For someone whose 300 pounds whatever's the case
Now were forgotten and goosed

For Sara

"Coming back"

A regret
Nothing more than purposeful
Memory
I had of you
Not acted upon, of course
Afraid to show weakness
Now buried with two souls
One living, one buried
Why did you go
Wendy Z.
Before I got to know you better
Sharing your commodious, feisty embodiment of something
I hope this restiveness lives on
The kind I saw in your eyes
For I'm still so engraved to this image
The strange retrospect and a sense
She knew me in another life and was coming back
Are words and letters to a grave
Ever returned
Well, I've had these premonitions before
After the facts of eventuality

Del Louis

"Falling"

Where I stand today
It's as if I'm kneeling
Like a raindrop
Dispersed
Falling, landed
That can't repel the object it struck
Or the crusader
Invading time or our minds
That I loosely scrap together
Like feathers to dead art projects
All innovation finished
Like a last kiss
As if we moved on from being a sorted
Possession
Just rubbish under a truss
The homeless might've more dignity
In a swill from the back of a commode
Holding a dripping candle
Purifying rough skin when it's touch cools
Dropped to my knees again
As if I were your fallen angel
Needled by God's unspoken words

"The useful pursuits of nothing"

Longing
Mind's uncoupled tow to desire
With all the particulars
As if it had to last forever
Longing before my creator / beast
Or someone I don't know yet
I can't wince
While the "Entourage" crew waits
Somewhere
Or just a girl
Like the nine sisters that are
Munificent
In a time of murkiness or need
Racked with pain, somebody say's

"Please don't go"

And the shadowy glow
Like angry embers of souls trying to crest
Lost in every flimsy hold on you
Because I wasn't emphatically ready,
To emit more charm
Making points of view clearer
So I shield away
From veld tomorrows
While longing controls me quixotically
Carrying it's trusted twisting plan
Unconsciously
To act on thoughts of expediency
The way Pandora did before
And Marlene in the adult film version
I'm thirsting to your cool mint lips
Before unintended maceration and time
Puts a quell on longing

"This soft rhyming rain"

The humidity
What a read on ABC, 60%
Felt like heavy sap
On my skin
Or the oil that basks
The air over Industrial
The kind that besmirch
Good clothes on any walk
But I was only stepping lethargically
Into my bathroom
Outside I could hear the rain
Orchestrating in rhythmic taps
Like the steady beat to
"Cruel to be kind"
Was God measuring all mankind
With these succinct beats of the rain
That assuages nothing to my thoughtlessness
All this curt rhyming
In cycles
Just like Paul Simon
Has done, each time his voice sounding
Freshly monotonously pleasing

"Woeful"

Soon, I'll be drowsed without authority
Before the dozen
Exercises her cruel crassness
With words like asshole
I turn like my draping cowlick and leave
Without any disputation
You can dissuade any human
But not ever the force of nature
When it rains it rains
Whilst customers become dissident
Over tapped beer where I sit
Waving their Tea Party flags
Or shouting "Hallelujah, Hallelujah
One man's misfortune
Another one's wrongful gain

"On a shift's end"

I've been dealt such a bad hand
It's like staring into dark molasses
At 12 am
When all you wanted was a glass of milk
Don't know where I stand in this world
Even corn has a silk casing down this road
Where a Myerstown truck stop restaurant
Only has milk cartons in quarter halves
Reminded me of the separation at
Birth when you're a twin
I'd rather wait for the dutiful waitress
Comfy in her sandals and a sheer
White halter top after her shift ends
Before turning down, toward
All the shanty dwellings on 422
That remind me of all that's lacking
And this liquor that readily calms
Now wracking the dexterity of my brain
Quieted down and lonely until you came
Breathing huddled below your scant bikini line
Before a night's final exultation

"Ripening"

Finally navigated
Past all your negativity without response
As if it was the vice grip of Satan imploding
Still you don't care about me
Or your own state so macerated
I can no longer slip further into your maelstrom
I've endured enough brutal chaos this time
Were not sailing
On the same main mast with a focus like Columbus
See my heart floating with the flotsam on waters
Foible as you made me
Above the fluke that ricochet on the bottom
Still could be lucky in love
Exiting a life as if it was gypsum made
When you come to your knee-jerk conclusions
Realize you had a k knavish heart
Except to the illegitimate ripe off-spring you rear
Kudos to your sensitiveness to them
I need no (repondez s'ilvous plait)
For I have grown past a seed or have huddled
Safely to someone's decay

"These ventures"

The cohesive tease of gambling
As if streaks or winning had no conscious
But it's template to euphoria
Or lasting solvency
And what if I lose
You see nothing ever changes much
I also gambled on someone
Not heirs for compatibility but also a future
And it seems every dream become somber
Like travelers of yore
Or sacred cows on ferry boats
Whose hearts were slayed in Conrad's novel
Where humanness had no fencing but a venture
To hardships and truths
That fog lasting memory

"Your glitter"

This head now plastering in
To my mind or full aging
With the help from Harp
But the look in your eyes
Is like the blistering gleam of fresh uncut flowers
With their pendulous swing in spring, ones that wait for
  adornment
And the sheepish, perfectible gaze of the sun
Past down
Blanketing or exiting my thoughts
Now all these faces but one that permeates a languid soul
Like a calm, forceful buzz Emily

"Appropos"

You keep feeling hidden and secure
As a talon before sapping
You must shellac all them you know
Excoriated me with curse words as if they were a shield
More even handed would be a maiden submitting
Who endures all this encumbrance in relations
But gains morality
Weighing on trust and the courage to deny me again, and again
All this to enhance my loneliness to…
As I beg for so little
Skin that covers all woes momentarily
Nothing enduring but the light of day, ever
With it's usual orchestration of denial letting all downgrade me

"What am essence"

Their line translucent
Felt pure as an electric nature
With defiance to change the subtle atmosphere
The beautiful sounds that reverberate
Off Edge and Keith
Little imitation plausible
Except their even temperament's glow, one we can't erode much
Like a stoic candle burning or a light breeze's touch
That stirs the will or the hair on a camel's back
Nils trailing in open tuning
As the moon quietly fastens to their sticking essence
To these immortals before dulling in time
Their lines before verse
A ring to independence or God seldom found niches
And fans still in queue
They were never in doubt staple as Marlboro or Fender
As our nature quibbles
The invisible line moves across the path of horizons
With a flared tempo and the grins of telepathy across stages
Every line holding back time
Painting themselves to paragon
Is it ever lonely or a stand-off
It's like a tide
Against an immovable fixture

"Dark beauty"

Beauty
Real or forged
Lastly becomes scoff or scourged
And I'm not counting the virtuoso's bend
On Pedro's torment
In his mind
Is it greater than the physical welts
Raised as the heat to rise above an ashen floor
Across from card-board lined windows
Below the glow of sirens some ravenous to johns
And a heart's silent howl
Courser the beauty not negating even in darkness
The girl in slip away outta anyone's earshot
She could've been your neighbor Jack
But when a knife becomes your nemesis
To crazies who can't neatly finish
Tracked beneath these dark valentines subterfuge
Some beauty is showed
In the opposites of what wasn't to be death
And all I can remember of her
Earnest in low rise jeans slinking way below a navel
Is inviting some kind of trouble if not careful
Some just can't be lucky to look
But some don't have a face or voice
While you stuck to the visceral
And everything becomes surreal
When imagery is a flow
To what's good

"Before dozing"

When I was a kid
I liked the passing sound of a train's horn
Down past Race St. or Moser
At midnight causing indelible thought and reverberation
Knowing I'm not alone in the long haul to deliver
And my eyes were closed covertly
To all the world's scorn as a mind relocates like freighters
Safely under a cover or quilt
Until the black steel marauder proceeded to pass if just to intrude
    sleep
Not ever knowing where I'm going, closer to inanimate objects
Skeptically keen as Sherlock at fifteen
Even fooling Patty, the babysitter without ones pro bandi
Not once, but thrice
Charm suffused without vanity or harshness

"These stars crashing"

The ungranted stars above
We counted on for direction
Came crashing hurriedly down
Like a blinding spur in sunlight
We were taken upstairs at 4pm
To a conference room
As lined symbols not names
Of someone's lionization
Eyes meek toward every commandant
And goons who stood near a door
We looked more lifeless
Than any mannequin
Before the news all were asked
To turn off cell-phones
Now I felt like the biggest yokel
To believe in an industry
Without representation of a union
And then we were fired, exploited for
Someone else's capitol gain
By insidious bastards with 3 initials
Who bathe in our oppression
Who call themselves – KKR
But don't labor laws only protect

The basic employer in PA
Who were any of us remiss
Cannot be proved by slipshod records
As I tried to dissuade a friendly manager
With a harrumph
Before a harridan grin
Freeing me from this omnipotence
To find ourselves again
Didn't you do me a favor
And I don't care about your prudence
Funny how someday you'll be taken aback
But you can't break me

"Pinning me"

You got me trapped
Like a pigeon on a granite ledge
Isn't it hard lapped to nothing significant
What doesn't your cold heart understand?
I can't be tied down to one thing so conventional
Your bearing no longer holds the right card
How many times was I renounced
And every vestige dulling as feathers
Felled in autumn waving in a wind pinned to grass and gravity
Without a whisper from anyone

Del Louis

"Wholly starling"

I use to walk thru the center city of Philly
Pretty girls with vague accents from the Southside
Grabbed all my attention without tripping or
Passer-bys from the train ride or just eclectic strangers
With green eyes and nice lashes
Or Lois with her nose ring and tight skirt
Blowing all that aroma
As if it was a latch-key to therapy or Les Gals on Market
All integrated to my being after awhile
As if we were the new beats or each-others attendants
Forming to all our craziness or intelligentsia
Motioning to a Starbucks
For black coffee or mocha with whipped cream
Pasting Linda's lips during every paused traffic light

"In a poem"

The final discourse
Had to be so curt I passed it on to another
Can you taste the curdle
Of dried up love in a poem
Now you know how the cutlass felt
Still, maybe you have no humanness or entrails
All was cut off at the source emblematic
To the other soluble God or hatred that
Was a passion to hurt me

"Passing"

What happened to the blind eccentric dozen at OFF track
I helped her thru the heavy glass door
Did she eventually break like a gentle wind
The kind that held you in an outdoor café
Anchored to a chair and a gentleman's charm
I watch a light breeze beating on an autumn leaf
As if it had a heart
And I thought of that old lady by herself and what must've been
Facing the helm of every singular day passing

"Something said"

What is left
When the bills are all paid
And the children are grown
And how many of us feign love
Some can't stay bereft forever
They have the energy of Tommy McDonald
And roam or move without caution
Like the wind against a battered sign
Some kid kicked too much
Or the farmer's vane that can't be measured in a cuckoo tempo
It reminds me of love when it's good and ferocious
Before it wanes
Like the moon in seasons remains like a furtive eye
But what is left to the aging process
My soul could profit from so little, going on
As ice curlicues around the young trees
I could offer those seventh graders coffee or cocoa
Traipsing off a bus or pavement
Before a news show comes on at 5:00 or Dr. Phil
What is really left but to tell them stories of yore
But always first ask something about themselves
They just might want to come in
Just to warm their mittens in this musty house
And make a curtsy

Before I tell them someone from the White Sox scandal
Was from Stowe
Surely, I don't understand or know what is left
But the kids might tell me of a Stones song they like off 'Exile'
Or how their into cyberpunk
While warming their lips to my cut-rate coffee,
Someone say's "I can see you sparkle with every answer
As if your mind dances with this convex wind." And this is the
      spot that remains
Where pre-teens sat on a hazel sofa with their ageless peer

"Washed away"

A squashed bug near a water drain
The borough ones with metal slits
And I might think of slim memory
That washed away
And how, friend, a life lost thru aging
Without much fuss
Flows like water down to find it's passage
Harder to find our intent to others ever
Or a friend
To stay some what intangible
As our lives interject to strangers who lend their time
Some of our favorite happy characters
We couldn't parlay
Past cheesy talk
Became like shadows thru those thin canals
In the pertinent parts of France
Now forever knowing
As the flowing pert reflective waters tell us
Nothing matters except impression less the depression left by
    deer on a knoll

"After I met you"

After our consensual mating
All the pulling off of spandex body suits
And more the seize on each-other
We made a comfy habitat
In our first general setting
A one-legged stripper livid across our divide
The best nuance to nearsightedness
Was the perched walnut trees drooping
Behind the kitchen windows
Or missy's fondness for Mustangs revving
The biggest nuance, I can't perceive is
Why the curtain in the bathroom stays closed in the dark
And I think of Janet Leigh's image in "Psycho"
And the other nuance
Is how a wife has to lay out kid's clothes before morning arises
These nuances have a numbing effect I can't put in numbers
Like the pot hidden in a bush in flames
If this meaning is off how in heaven do I change her tone
It's like being in retort with a failed systems analyst

"Hunger"

Your mellow eyes
That look of longing, the hunger
To lost endearment not yet discernable
You could've met an enfilade to a heart
Your eyes like a squid dead on ice too
But then you light a cigarette
And encroach on to something
During our conversation your lips as sweet as sorbet
Few who I met are so engaging
Then you absorb me by breathing even when you smile
Thru that look of longing with query that I touched on
And your hair another cynosure
Brushed away all those burrs
When you were holding the cosmos
Strong as the crispy crème stars that shined
We were both coterminous

For Courtney

"What destiny is"

Does anyone know what destiny is?
What it is we can't make better any interpretation
Is better left to imagine you
Destiny is what I didn't do or take yesterday
Give me a memory that last
Stay longer than a penetrating sun
One that glistens past/on to my soul
Unto many tomorrows
With that sweet pungent stout aroma
That baste the air I breathe
Like beer gardens in late spring
Destiny is what I thought you would be
But you don't trade in black markets
Deceptions like mercury masks
The before-hand assumption that I would know you
Now a split card in a deck
The one that fans time
Before we become destiny's rigged proponent
Were we born of makeshift love

"Proof of"

Sometimes things come to me
At the most precise moments
As if there is some kind of reprieve
Is this proof from God, a retort
As we become reshuffled from the masses
Back to something good
And behavior all in toot, mastering our domain
Before the final horn's blast
When I was down to my last bet
Rooting for Montana, Johnny V.
Or Chamberlain Bridge
Was it because I was besmirched in misery
And life's dreariness
I couldn't drop kick clean
Except in premonition or dream
And to think we act presidium over all
As sometimes things come to me
So abstractedly
How could I know walking past a black car
That's it's driver was related
To a neighbor I've met thrice during these errand runs
She said, "My sister's waiting outside and I can't come over"

"Byway"

What is in a name, anyway
Some of my relatives I've never met from the west
Don't criticize others idealisms
All families have wanderers in them
One man choked off his immediate one
The grand father I never knew or his children
We must've took from him to be a fancier
I don't know what to say in Jack's memory
Was he a beat hook in retrograde
Do I carry any of his synchronous traits!
Did he ever met Kerouac
In San Francisco's rail yards?
Is he keeping tabs on us
Rootless and so bootless from the grave
May be the border line of a name

I'd probably be at peace
If I could see you one more time
You wouldn't be faceless
Before aging makes us unrecognizable
Christy could set us up if just to talk crazily
About how we rose into our own
Maybe we didn't without the slopes
And never knowing you again
Would be more awful than cousins and niece's living close who
    don't come by
I never needed an explanation of why you left me...
Except to be in others clutches
The need
I'm a grown dope you see and I can't possess a thing
But a will that travels
You took the trip to trajectory
Did you find it was better?
Why am I asking? Because the heart stings
As if you covered me in your dead ashes
And still you lay at my heart that remembers
How exclusive we were

"Some budding effect"

She asked me what day it is;
The way I asked the same thing
A cell phone would indicate,
Along with terse filled messages
I couldn't resurrect to something
Called sin / but friendships are allies
And I'd cross this indefinite terrain without thinking it over
We put bold emphasis on dates
Timed as Randy Moss on route
As if dates had some great reckoning
More so to a plan of schizophrenics
And because of them I'm unsettled as numbers to their order
     growing dim
When time passes us

"Just listen"

If I could hear what nature's thinking
The way children do with conch shells
That sound the roar that could purge all mankind
But just listen
Just maybe the stillness of night so rarely object
Could solve the riddle of my life bound
Before more deriding by others
Who paint a canvas of their own caustic pain
But nature's way is to complain
Without any enumeration we sorted through to
And I felt the pangs of swirling trees bowing like dragons
The same way dogs do before the outbreak
Of nature's calling closes in
Telling me nothing is quite understood
Not even break-ups and devastation

"Creeping to Normalcy"

Ordinarily,
We use to have a routine
That I would call our genuine age of innocence
When you closely resembled a gem to me
Your legs and hips, breasts
Would oscillate against your partner
Making him happy and orgulous
Now all that staved away
By child rearing of grand children and menopause;
We may all have an aversion to aging
But you did little to change
Where was your concentration to me
To what ourselves know later is wisdom and truth
Some never get
It seems you really wanted me to hate myself
But I can't grovel to your low self-esteem
And what our daughter ought to do doesn't
Building a life so nefarious and lame
When your family turns on you completely
As a tire blown
It's time to leave on the beat train
Maybe I'll visit the train yards of Minneapolis
Over fluff clouds
The one's extolled by Dylan in thought or portrait
So I don't have to figure out
Why you have an aversion to sex
It's like it is, was for us now
Something expedient, fading
Like soap suds in a washer,
Cycling to languor and a finish
As I relinquish all bad feeling
What was it that was ordinary

"Think"

I don't want to be alone tonight
Is another anniversary of nothing special
Alone is alright for some with meadow thoughts
Who've lost the balance of passion
Vixens don't need to vivify any substance to a man
Still she's reveling from her child-hood
Caught in her mind's vortex
Maybe only what's chiefly voluptuary she needs
Alone with the grooved wood furniture
And the collie ruffled against his plush carpet
All that's left that is consanguineous
And I still think of an embarking, equable tomorrow
Where we sat under shaded trees with their armor
Eating wine sap apples
With all that charisma of yours
Cleaving to my knee and nestled
As if you were begging for chastisement
And then you laughed
Stirring the mallards
As if they were in restraints
Coughing up their own words as I forgot to say,
"Thanks for being so humane."

"Night-time"

The day retreated into darkness
As if a painter stripped base color
And nature's quietude never a travesty
As stillness sounds in my mind
Except for some black tread over asphalt roads
The few drivers withdrawing from a heyday or spirits
Buzzing by so crickety
And you with your pressed lips
And soft fingers against my skin warming
Peeling away my essence
As if night-time was just another wanton escapade
While a silvery moon shined through my window
Before swooping like geese to an astral plane
We could never envision
We were two birds embolden to the sky

"Those fancy imprints"

I remember telling a friend how real effectual change usually happens or a hankering to when were past thirty before middle age. You see something in your mind before feeling any infirmity to one thing and know not all things or relations are finite in life. And who hasn't been down that road before and aren't we really propelled by our own inertia, and lost time.

How many times have I told someone when were at our peak and can be no more fertile to someone it's time to go on? How many relationships are still swelling up after twelve years? I really felt this infection after raising a teen, as if there was more purpose, more love to give. I stayed past this seventeen year curve through all the pain and anguish not all a physical kind of all that was indomitable, such as having an immature, indolent daughter. One who acts so self-serving and narcissistic even though she has a thyroid problem. And without the proper continuous con-selling remains ineluctable.

How could I after all this time and an awakening of the soul not go after what's true or most meaningful to ourselves? And they all say pain does subside or do we or lovers keep it buried until sepulcher almost the way Patricia Neal almost did. Although Lindsay and Sam should reenact some kind of pact. Time doesn't have to open old wounds. We can repel from it, smile, and move on.

Any time, maybe soon we meet suddenly our immaculate partners. The one's you pass on macadam parking lots. The one with the small imperfections you find so charming. Those small freckles eluded by a falling sunset crossing piercing hazel eyes, and the whitest skin. What would we be if not for chance would make us more fallible.

And those fancy imprints of the mind of all imagined dream can become real, if we believe we have the capacity to grasp and hang on to something even if it starts with the stern that dashes breathlessly like I did out of enchanted rooms. Or stayed close to enigmatic patrons. And to feel the silky stillness of Emily's resources behind me with a sweet enjoin saying "guys I won't be at Hof Brae this week end. I'm going to visit a friend on long island. And she said it so endearing, we laughed us guys. I must admit she helped during this pivotal period of growing and then moved on like Chabon's mysteries. To now not knowing what is better a beginning or an end.

Does life have to be so endemic as plants or trees

"What you read"

When you read each profound pronunciation
So amazing that look of concernment
As if you were afraid or wincing from some truth
Sized up like a cannon
Maybe each word reflective
Or a deflected promise
The willies Arthur Miller must've felt to
Hoping for some propagation
But reached for the pen instead
Mightily in you I found foremost a brevity unexplained
Like clouds in cover before they formalize each day
With your conciseness I can afford
Even in t hose 240-second boiled poached eggs
Silky and buttery pulled to a fork
As I slowly begged for more

"River of thought still running"

Even in less happy times
You are now just a vague imprint
But I don't do impressions
Even of myself
Because I'm forever changing
Subtle as the changing leaves falling
I could tell you, one time
A river flowed behind the plant on 7th Ave. West
Just ask "Joe" or any long time resident
I could tell by how long banks look like pews
And in-between them
Like a pressed phantom hand into a water's basin
Where now only grass stands
Bogged down by our own evolution transitory
Easier to just know I'm dogged by perverse thoughts
You may have of me wheeling around
Or any lasting impression sought to authority
Is blood's cold rush in winter on a lonely dark path
To get yourself past this indifferent wrath
One you could never feel

"I'm here"

Will you remember me
Beyond the provoking after I've gone
And not do self-indulgent things
That please initially and hurt soon later
Just think
But can't you feel me and all I've said
Lines you like elastic
Or that stringy stuff made for Halloween's webs
Spirited to
Know I never left this plastic world
I'm here always
For you to build on my impression
Even if it seems the flake beside the mirror
Roughly where you stand
With every innuendo inside you now
Flashing back to me
As if I were a whimper on a blade of grass
Only insects could listen to

"Descending"

Sunday, June 05, 2011 just like the rest of the week's slow
    decline
As the beaker drops each solemn tear
Nobody dared or showed
Waiting, waiting, waiting fearless
Like the flowers with nothing to do before spring
Didn't even catch one breath of you, peripheral and
Soldering into tomorrow's dream
Without one hint of dismay

322

"In decorum"

I could call you a schlep
Would that be flatteringly cynical enough
The beauty in your humility like a snail's
Is it's isolation
All this too hard to challenge
Affords us better relations
And it's silence like hunched flowers
Over stone formed from humus
Prouder as when we talk of talking
As if were trapped in mountains
Your so modest to limitations
My own ego can't see only what's unobtainable
This ingenuous humility shining
As if it's wisdom is the purse
Makes you innocuous to any scrape
And we haven't yet
Touched the set mizzen drapping below the skyline
Where there's waters we humbly ignore
Because nothing is as pertinent as ourselves.

"Slowly"

I let existence become clouded and muted
Like a soft caressing wind blends slowly to
Something we can't equate
Carried the lurid grave dancers of a past
Slowly now and multi-tasked to their senses
Across the Cineplex and two rusted freight tracks
You could almost feel their anxiety and move
As a leaf wavered on a tree where we walked
And all the others still as night, must be "Linda" G
As one whispered as in motto
But I didn't see a mask or human figure, how ho-hum
Nearing to Halloween
I stayed stripped and shallow
Without having means
Is a soothing quality
Just waiting to rise above all meritocracy
You see it is the simple things that our minds endure without
    betrayal
Those wine sap apples
Clutched to a basket
Later washed down with micro-brew
And the spiraled sunset over San Diego
Keeps me holily sincere
As the fretting quiltess slowly spins her needle

"Almost no one"

No one calls me by name
As if words would threaten
Allegiances to a him or her
Without a name there's no placation
Maybe I'm not their brand
No one to call my name
Is so alien
To my way of thinking
And the need to have to others
A long surpass of tradition
No one calls me by name
Not even after a trusting surmise
Or that idyllic hug so twined
That Twain easily could bestow
Even if I act or talk idiomatically, but
Chrissie, called me by my name
The girl from the nondenominational
Church along Sanatoga
Like an angel waiting on every Shore front
Is as coincident even to me
As we sat handsomely in tedium

"Passing thru"

Pass where I'm going
Leave no hint or tire mark
Maybe like reading Braille
When I can see
Where I'm going randomly
Move to the gravity of mindful defiance
Or nothing
Or a place non-gratis of course
Now all these stops between brevity / and
Where I'm going before a slight rest
Turns to yesterday's ashes lay scented
But you were burning in-between visits, weren't you
Before the first endeavor
Met the gratitude of longing
Where I'm going I don't quite know
Before you were born ancestral karma had created
A hedge between us, now moved by time or pity
But where I'm going consciously is so trudging as life is
I'd rather pass into Lancaster, PA.
Before Lancaster, CA.
Jame's the directions weren't in the novel
And how do I propose to get to Akron, OH.
When I'm passing a sign on (222) for Akron, PA.
Is a shorter distance between entity
Believe it or not it may intersect Intercourse, PA.
And it's people
Before I turn
Off the veneer roads
Some that a crystal imagination imbibe to

"What's said in words"

Comfy words in ink resting on pages
Even Hunter's dogma
Some with a soliloquy to ourselves
Likened to the telepathy of band members meticulous on stage
Knowing their woven spots
It's as if they correlate to our pulse
Each letter similar to our corpuscles
Corked to our minds
As if were reaching for something worth living for
Muscled to our world in constant defiance
So I read, read, read

"Passing" (Pt. 2)

Could've cut thru every pointing chord
Even beauty's malocclusion
Every tigress showing slight malice
Why, even you
Now no words as if they were arms without proper targets
Or some malady
Can you feel me close, far away always hinting
Or are you treading time quietly "passing"
Like waste to a compost before expansion
Wrest away all that's significant
And no longer can I rant about it's loss
Tickling me like a tussled wave brushes and subsides
Eventually making all sadness clear without perception
Still cutting thru before the here after incites like a riot me or
    you
Wind swept as yesterday's tone was more tolerable feeding back
Every remnant that made you
Tepid as swans at spring time

"Finding reason"

Being jobless is not without cause
But leaves you stained to others self-centeredness and pomp
To be ignored like this, reprimand isn't enough
As if the working coiffure loss but I am still reputable
As the homeless guy is, with a sheen in the sun
See me, feel repulsed, remember I won't simply go away as a
    fading memory does
Being jobless doesn't resonate well with the working class-less
They don't know how it feels to be free because their resolved to
    brain washing
So tactical to economy's growth margin
But being jobless can be rootless or centered and still pitiful
If we don't try new things
Much less stripping dignity before finding a new tact or posse
Removing this fruitless tag
Being jobless isn't secondarily the worst thing
Is like covering a bottomless hole
As each patriot to is destined to the left
The grief is just to leaven and the soul is to gratitude
Found only in one dilettante
Saved you compliments with a meaning now so joined

"Groundless"

Delbert,
In a place of confinement between Victorian walls
With thinning compressed air
Of a languid toad who hangs by a thread on a lily pad
Still indefatigable as I am
To dicker with this clan to find meaning
Like the satirist David on planes with hipsters
Ain't it ironic
When sadness tools a beginning somewhere
To find harmony without levy
As you become gracefully hoary
Can't lose a little more needing someone to hinder all aging
And Hillary squashing my sham and harmless fun
Because she's cleverly cunning too, texting a fool
Truth is a pun, beauty is hoodwinked it shackles pride
You hopscotch thru inn's so hospital to customers you know
As you bravely encamp to others
See, she's gawky with disdain and smarmy
It would be disparaging trying to court her
Someone fertile as a cowbird
When she see's your losing ground
Caught in a sunset's sloping gauntlet
Racing to find a reason with a 100-to-1 odds
Is oddly appealing
When all that's left is my persistent charm
Even when I can't size you up
You remain perky in abandon
As I lose faith in the human race
Dallying before being countersunk by our youth
To be shamelessly groundless

"Illusionary quest"

In every solid state
Of all life's affairs
Just a warmed over myth that love can bring
And bliss is just for fairies over 54-inches tall
Might as well be Stiff-ler
Pissing off a balcony's ledge so perfectly
And in-between with soft dew lap
Where beautiful skin was once placed
Now so much easier to devolve, somersault to balance
Maybe I can solve some of tomorrow's uncertainty without being
    solicit
Tom-boys make weskit wingmen at that Irish pub
With that topaz hair that Jen has under a toque
Tomorrow's dream was tomahawked way back in 94'
Stopped like a rock disintegrates blasting down a hill's crest
Can I get past all the tumult and know what's best
Is it simply too late to care when reality is stronger than fiction
Shared a doobie on the fire-escape with God
And thought briefly that all is steeped to societal woes that
    sunder
As we sat soporific and clenched like an emulsion's stain
Two tears so encrusted as one entity in the bleach of autumn
Wary to find a lasting shtick to encompass your heart
As you danced briskly between the black wrought iron
Wrest away all the fear of …..

"Leading to"

What kind of life have we led
As if were composed a betting criminals, no less
Who crisscross the yellow-tape caution mark
You feign aptness no sooner could we become grafters
Scrapping up bar tip money for food
All faith becomes broken as twigs
Readying for kindling
As love became an infirmity
I still searched for hope and my soul's inevitable graceful
    surrender
Was to tomorrow's innumerable passion
To the insipidity of our nature
Likened to watching cattle graze along Elverson
Who see us a cat's paw with stealth plans
But you walk so proud Grafin
As if wearing Berber jewelry or carrying pieces of Krugger and
Staunchly in your pockets
As our hands closed together steely cold at first
It became a star like night
Steadfastly geared to nothing
Until the morning sparrows called out two deer stood stationary
Transfixed to their taste buds or my stare
Huddled in our parked car as if we were twined to your inseam
Guiding me past any turpitude
Twiddling to be stark
Over a pending watching quieter moon

"Swaying"

The comfort of the hammock
Under the bending walnut trees
Soon life will switch
Without my knowing
Hijacking tomorrow or low-bred you
Splitting time like a hobo hitched to a train ride
Abides by no rules that would hinder
A lamp maker or coppersmith
The sway so contrary but concise as saying,
"Let's go."
And the compensation so lovely
Encroaching the left in the garage
As your feet pitter-patter on the ladder
I eye your figure's sway or curse
And it's impertinence of imprinted memory
Like dissolving ivory snow
Is now just a single tare
And I can't bear losing sway
The kind that governs festal tap-rooms
Of the otherworldly
And equating fools that try to pin someone else's imagery

"Falling"

As most vivid desires are elusive daydreams
No wonder we fall apart
We can't be nature's undivided seas with their seams
Thrusting on measure to shorelines
Where's thoughtful minds can't see the receding of earth
Were obsequious to
Still we fell apart to say the least
All the hipster or yuppies I could consort to then
All that's contemplative without plans
Something finally conterminous and social
What I can't resort to most
The list would be endless
As revelers marching to Mardi-Gras
And I found out this isn't no fun anointed by Shrews'
And what I can't resort to most:
All the indiscipline you rely on to others
Nothingness the kind that holds you firmly in place
As the weathered post the wind beats
What about the despoils
Of all that was desirous, gone, gone, gone
And on all the buzz to some culture
Still you are killed with ennui
As something to do
Go back to your source
Where you belong
I can't bear to watch
The slow, silent descent of happiness
When I'm falling beyond
Reproach

" "

When I just started cracking
Without a break
Your smile, words so soft
Like liquid sunshine on my brain
Releasing dopamine
Now I can't shatter most myths
Things got worse at fifty
Didn't find someone cool, swank, and nifty as Jen was
Then the world crashed
Twice since 911
And then big money never bats a lash
What am I deferred to
More loss, until Obama makes his cuts
Couldn't live forever on pot luck
Shackled and shocked to all this
The harvest of tomorrow isn't all unknown
Caught all your infused spark
Before waning begins
The sound of BO's crackling firm chords on our dial
As the sun leaks thru
A sylph
Firmly placed beneath me
Without a red wood expression

"Preserving"

I've been meaning to write you
Again
With a fore-cast
Nothing is sent on your behalf
I keep volumes of you
Like I'm shedding skin or shiny wheat
Quieted words from myself preserving
Selflessly in love with your image
Like the first time we met so clumsily and dashingly proud
Now my mind rarely commutes
To anyone
In that ethereal place we lost
Bidding to the unknown quest
Gone so far away
When we could've been like beads flashing together
Wrapped around flesh

"Favorite one"

I saw you again
You were standing as if you were compressing air looking
    fortuitous
With your arms crossed at Midas
You had on a red sweater I remembered before
I didn't know it was you, still and mulling
Until my car passed thru
The reality of
Sending some cosmic scenic beauty forward
Did you see me?
If then were you swept by passion's throes;
Suppression and our gilded breaths
As is all our lives
The best and worst theatre

"As I roam"

I watched disconsolately aware
As bone met that Bachman pretzel you ate
Felt the knowing discomfort
Of all we can't afford to fix or change
Easier to re arrange a puzzle
Didn't get the new glasses
Since the last eye exam in February
Or a warm sweater for the next February in 11
For all those cold days of winter that mask
Pennsylvania
As rangy as I am why don't I get these things done
Maybe I'm just looking to be more
Rapaciously drawn to longing
Where character precedes envy
Somewhere I find tumbledown dignity
Inside ourselves
Hidden like layered shelves of slate
On hillsides where a spring ran
But who am I rambling to
Rambunctious ghostly patrons of yore
Swallowing the last bits of my Reisling
That I washed down with mountain dew
Because I only had $1.50 left on Mastercard's plastic
And all I've found is a world without elasticity
Egregiously to all I've grown up to
And then there's Christy soft as a wind of change

"Roaming" (to)

Don't want to wake up to
Another prickly dream
Investing in what's completely emotive
Although I roam like a waif without clarity
One who can't come home
How can we be so pleasant and defiant
At the same time without a scheme
We could've waded thru all that's vexing
But that became non-descript as paint colors
And I'll never get the real picture's meaning
So give me lord a dirty blonde
One with a slight dredge of freckles
And hair that looked so sparkle
Where we trampled between the
Ivory
And the early shoot of spring
That reciprocates some kind of empowerment
Until we reach the emollient car seats
Before freshening for tomorrow's plan
That light could frisk
For once things don't looks so moot
Under the mountain ash
You made your proposal
Before darting like a sylph

"Indomitable"

For two days
The sun looked like obstructed graying patches
Of civil war casualties
Pinned against an albumen sky
General Chamberlain leaned against a porous boulder with a
    cigar
As nature stood motionless indomitable
With it's placidity watching over all
Peeling us down to halves
And I don't have one good memory
At the end of this decade
Fading back to some youthfulness
Moving on against an unneighborly world
Dodging a whisking arrow's crossbow across from scented
    honeysuckle
Where we stood pleated in arms, smiling
Buckling beyond enamor
As the sparrows song in their far off district
Encased to their simple madness

"Changing"

If love is the greatest risk
Then why do we implore to take it on
To be complete and magnanimous
Is to become for flung over the cliff or deck
To a meringue foamed sea
When it is over, rallied to freedom
Then I stood under a meniscus moon
Changing it's picture daily
Lest nature souls over take what we had
The best days before middle-age
Now I feel sadly deprived as you in a voiceless keen
Still can't kaput this rage or passion
Might fill up a room for two
As the maverick in me roams
Ceaselessly and flamboyant too
All flashiness just a memory
To holding you
Was a gallant fight to maturity
Now what's next to attest
Sooner children get older
And I need a bold form of
Contentment
For the roles we play

"Comparing"

It's so hard sometimes, Hilda
To tell the difference between a cold, flu symptoms
And these allergies
Someone called a doctor, or (A,B,C.), say's
"If it lasts longer than a few days it's the later."
To me it's like comparing girl-friends
Without knowing each-other's quirks or body composition
Some leave keels on during sex
And yes some want that flagellation with it's burns
To be reddened like from poison ivy
No worse than a flushed face with fever
But if you just have a cold
You can divide getting the flu before February
Watching the naked snowman with the carrot for a nose
And all these concerns are deserted when we get well again
Now I can abandon a blonde at will
For a eclectic, steamy brunette
Named collette
Who braids her hair in small spots
I asked her what ailment she prefers
Before our ravishment unfolds;
And she say's, "don't kiss me, I have a cold, just a cold."
As if she's praying for sick leave
To wiggle her toes freely under a tucked blanket
Or curl her fingers into a plush pillow nearing her torso
Really not that much different than me
Coddled to Fox News before eleven

"Just karma"

If you look to far into my bloodlines
Don't be surprised to find just a few links
Could be like a changing molecular phase
But when you talk about mom saving a bird
It's as if we had a constellation and accord
Juxtaposed when you were young before you knew me or were
    born
A karma that spread like wind to bluegrass and abroad
Is this just self-conscious pompous gratification I concealed
Tell me
I'm a seer who just sees a semblance to something so selfless
Thanks for interfering making your own call
For all that proposed origin I messed
You can't interfere with fate
Might be the plan we waited for
Or am I truly lost at last

Del Louis

"the last prospect"

The prospects of tomorrow shelved
Like the ball player stuck in the minors
Segregated from reality playing a game
Moving thru shanty country towns I can't pronounce
Their girlfriends wait stoic and stodgy
For the slugger's arm
For late night fun and rocks in fancy tumblers
Before a bus or plane takes them to another horizon
As I'm felled by loss or simple routine
Is only a beginning of true awareness
As more mushroom clouds form
Through an allotted bogus sun today
Stripping plans away like rotted dry-wall
And the one last desire I had
And the one last desire I had
Before that guy's game is rained out
As if by God's design
Was to see you again
The time we had better than a kid's first glove

"Pressing"

You were once pressed to my heart
Like a shiny cellophane dress
That black horse riding the biased rail
With streaks of blonde coiling in the air
Why I didn't pursue this challenge remains unseen;
But still burns
A hole thru our patched lives and scars
The hardened truth I circle with caution
And you hide shameless behind that shield
Caught the rails umpteenth to Deluth
And I thought of that trader John Wilkes Booth
Now loosely my spirits remains
Like a cracked fault line imploding in Northridge
Did I lose that space in your heart
Without a wiring
This whole futile search becomes secondary
When you choose to be on a pace by yourself
Dusting all in that path

"In 100-days"

Anthony G. of the morning show
Tells the professor that stats don't matter
This time they didn't to our Phils
Red P Fight ins rebounding core is a fear
Spreading once again in April 2011
Now revered enact by the 8 degree mark
As if we were sparked in flames of temperance
· The ones that lead to grace nobody sees
Most of the times numbers are relevant
To being masterful as Koufax was fire-balling to fame
Or minimally horrendous at the Mendoza line
There are those among us thinly crafted survivors
And in time slanting migratory birds return to replenish – in 100
    days.

"Showing you off"

Can you remember
How I use to show you off as if you were art
By doing simple things
The walks in parks so perfected crafted
Almost empty while Dorney's in season
With curling lakes whose waters look lacquered by evening's
    lights
With men in uniform made of shiny metals
A fire place and benches for two, even a white stage with steps
I use to show you shirts from Slack Shack in my closet
Just to get you alone in that cuppy room
To begin the slow undressing to foreplay
Took a knack when you wore a spandex body suit
Or was that to show your out a-bounds
To share you with this world even in the seventies was a risk and
    gamble
I took to a calm temperament
I use to show you off without a purpose
As if you were a bouquet of flowers
Waving in the opened motorcade beside Jacqueline Kennedy
Now I just want to show you off-once more
As you vitality wanes to be useful
Now I just want to show you off
To see if anyone could be committed to
What I lost
Is faded, faded like a rose

"Intermingle"

Judy
Stop beating yourself up
For what happened before
Wasn't sagely refundable, debate the paste
Regale in the pleasure
Of the unknown if you can
The way Verne and Voltaire did
Redirect the tide of your soul
With embracing
The way snow folds on hickory
Don't sabotage every new chance today
With every puzzling text sent allotted
I see someone w hose so punchy, cooby
Merge closer to my purest center, please
Before the somel light fades to winter
And the winds snarls against them outside
Without much guise to anything, know
I don't care about your background or it's agenda
So good me to instruction, make me feel alive
Because dreams are only mementos to hunger
So let's dig a milepost one we'll stay close to

"Truly know"

The best things I know
Those vague self-comprehensions
That have eluded us all
As if were living half truths
Are we true to ourselves if we don't pursue what we want most
And what happens when we find it's
Cracker jack surprises
Something safe as happiness hung in someone's mind
Like a fastened Christmas wreath
What happens if she leaves? You
Would it destroy the rounded motion of time,
That romance brings?
When I was trying to be my true self
All I found was a steady positioning to God
The only cushion that's real
When I'm dogged and logging to loneliness
As I lay on cold sharp steel rails
Looking into your hazel measured eyes
That shadow and mask an early departure,
As you said, "Please hold on."
I'll sheer the fear inside you, truly
Know I am here to vanquish every painstaking journey

"Flavery"

When will I find someone
As soft as Winona or flower petals
Pressed to my heart
With a back narrow with slitted grooves against ribs
Fine as the swift
One or two things still on my bucket list
But I could never twist a mind
When I had a simple need
That wasn't mastered to proclivity
I had to find one
Profuse as my grandmom
With eyes so peerless as chestnuts
That see the truth in all ancestry
Pressing to my heart
As if were an obtuse branch on a tree

"Nov 2nd"

When Tuesday comes
It'll be 32-degrees outside
When many languid incumbents
Get thrown under the bus by voters
Now maybe someone can invest in our freedoms
Once more
With new founds indigenous growth
Say good bye to dirty laundry Soros
At least we'll give you an indelible sun
Tuesday's elections on Nov 2nd
Only a day God could make
With so much dissent and much rake
Why do the laws of the constitution
Have to become multi-sense?
When it should be for all and one for legals
And I almost forgot in 48 hrs
I'll get a dime's worth of redemption
And still be forgotten by almost everyone
How can I now ever find an ounce of rectitude
Anywhere
As in the red-eye and a cheap room
Called The Waverly Inn, so legendary
Where girl's swoon to soak up drinks
Like a wet swathe
And then move like the water strider
With their wavelet curls and curves
When, and if I had their nerve to ascend
Hope I don't become more denigrated [unreadable]

"Hinting to"

As a child without seeing
Tried to think many things
Thru at once
But were hot-wired all of us
Turtles may even know more
Than a young dunderhead
Now as I age fluidly
I still try to do many tasks at once
As if to forget all the dusting
By others
The meager, attractive waitress
Who said, "I can't".
Wavering from the check sent
Back
As if I were a beast with -3 numbers
And that dilettante edging to her
Dynasty
As if she could suck a diamond-back whole
Why is it? I have to dicker
To lesser
Even the aromatic smells of
Yeast
Currying in an oven
The place Plath rested her head
Inside of
Lastly one of impudence

As all insecurity builds and
Wanes
Until you gave an innuendo
In-so-far as a blink or a wave
Affording a day and a half of
Shade under quilts with rural
Scenes
When we could feign
All that's insuffereable at
Motel 8
You made plausible
All I could settle for
Calming as a still river

"Leading to"

The light of day
Like a brigadier general's demand
Bringing all our weaknesses together
Where we sit huddled like white stones
Beaten like baked meringue
Knowing dreams are just snippets
Or half truths on the mend to tarot readers
And I wondered what happened
One time professed to boldness
How I played Chamberlain Bridge
Not to reign supremely
Resisted some pain
As Tess played with her bangs
Peering out the window
For our image was merging
The way wind curls on water
Menacingly leading us to vagueness
And the stillness which is life

"Blending"

I was on the verge of knowing
Our love was unfolding
Like the lilies held waiting at the finish line
That once blended against forestry
As I embolden you to
Another erotic escapade
All things with few
Furrow nearby to connected aliens
While we took things further
Merging like two smooth sails

"These subtle signs"

Marked each day reserved
As a sandbag firmly holds
Forcibly edged to a shore
And I felt so lagging without you no expedience to try
Swore I couldn't wait any longer on life
The change I see comes within boldly underlying some little
    truth
Nether when I was lonely
Happier to alter any image every dalliance
Needs foolery to shun
Someone whose lapsing
As if something's out of helter

I even see the leaves bristling in December differentiate quietly
Making mad waves
Can't change like the seasons that hopscotch away
Who could see my future better than Jen
Every sign or mark of nature more real than the hokum displays
    human's make
[unreadable]

"Cream dream"

If your waiting as I am
For a silver lining
I'm not a prince of oil
With denominations
I was dethroned of middle-class rank
Felt the dent of an imploded economy
Where big money went for blood shed
Stained every blue-collar dream
And moved forward jet-streaming
Hokey how GM and others bounced back
Soldiering
We became a mass of societal
Freaks
Working minimally to survive
Flimsily, some not at all
So shared one of opacity
If your looking for a silver lining
Don't solicit me till I find paradise
My 401-K nose divide on a flare
And I had no spare to run
Now I'm thin as a flat fish
Where do we find omnipotence once again
Flee for the fields of Italy
We could grow olive trees, pull ox carts
Hide out with Don Johnson in a villa
Smoking Monte Cristo no. 2
Was this just a phantasm
To heaven's portal
Smell the harvest of sweet onions
And basil over sauce begging for a
Palate

"Paling to"

Paler then the masses
Or you wanted me to be
Shackled in a padlock of despair
Did they want to thwart
All who had promise and were palpably true
As a palomino or man
Were close to a shadow gov't so omnipotent
More real is a tea party caucus assault
Can they foil the elite proliferation
And I fought to be prominently yours
Could've shared in all that is wickedly in this
World
Someone to be there without demand
When the web of socialism crept on all shores
We smiled and held hands standing
In the face of adversity
Like the liberty halves
Did we mistake hokey power for vision
Before a sun's burning fluorescence foils
With a combinant red sea and roaring trumpets
That hearken the true
While we grazed before a rural setting
As if we were groupies
Guided by nature's subtleness
Paler is the cream curtain's curling
In front of a beach-front condo
And your swirling hips and torso in tempo
To "The Kills"
A symbol of fixed divinity
More real than the afore mentioned delusion
Of the Soros' gang entrenched to a myth

"Tender"

If notes are only desperate attempts of
Dating, Here's one:
I was busy just thinking of you
Driving, doing errands
Knowing I can't keep my likes
Trying to find complete equability
In everything I do is a tender
Just a ghostly pine to hear your
Voice again

"Playin for pay"

The price we settle for
Not to be the caricature of
The mainstream trap
That shears roots with little
Severance
But words sewed on the underground
Priceless and perfected to you
Like the beauty of quartzite caves
Dad use to crawl thru in York some quadrilateral as home plate
We stamped with Adirondack bats
Playin for Town Toy decked in green
Waiting for Coke and pretzel rods
Across from Firestone
When we were teenagers
Maybe more suitable to flirt
With the neighborly sitter
When the parents were away

"Skywriter"

Suzie's skin
The fervor of white molded blossoms
I waited almost 20 yrs for that perfect skyline frame
And it's homogenic path of cream
Over Utah or Gotham
Only to find anonymity
The wrath of graying matter clouding judgment
But bones and ashes rise like the Phoenix
In these tilted time frames
You lasted afforded me
Our coupled pretense patently placid
That something gilded could be better
And it was
Even the kisses so peachy and Absolute
To absolve this writhing
And, oh that waistline flat as a white sail
Shimmying down like a vested moon
Over darkness
And by late morning above me the scant gray skywriting
That says, "T&T"

"Without cause"

The world's openness
Where only perquisite crows lay
And it's humble traps
Look at earth worms on side-walks
Flooded out of rich soil
Hovering until their a dried hardened shoelace
And humans built to sustain and absorb
Constant insults
From insular heads of power
One's you can't get even with or face
Because of protected labor laws
The law of the land changing
Now to make us smaller and weaker
Is a humbling prospect
Not ever to be able to prosper
But every trap has a hidden door
To lavish settings and their effect

"Untimely"

Untimely
Trumpeted sounds and then
Whispers
Before mayhem and final
Persecution or life so infinite
Or the last refraction
Of a sun or smile
On a shared hill
That teases awareness
Before a regnant God
I had to tell you something
"stir and resuscitate
This restive love
Proud as Geronimo and
Festive cubs
And the peering stars
That watched us
Like a plain clothes-man on
Guard
Whilst the seldom seen playgoer claps at closing time

"Ann Margaret"

Scorching the silvery screen
In my youth of discovery
Seen later harrumphing
Grumpy old men with whiskers
Who talk about nothing or what was once
We could harangue about her,
Forever
The soft sweetness of her voice
Velvety as chocolate
That sensual siren
With no slackness
And those two, you know
Resting below a neckline
Ann,
So comely as a single snowflake at dawn

"Smoothing"

Outside –
The wind provoking
Every unused thought in stupor
With a wild strike zone
Stirring like a swizzle stick to a drink
Roaring like a lion before sinking his teeth
And the amazement of tomorrows
Unknown lean gains
Stringy as the walnut offshoot
Beside the rusty resident cars auburn stain
At the body shop dying for repair
Or for kids to break in with caution
Every blurred thought now just a wrinkle
From the winds blow smoothing
On the face of a pond
I passed in Elverson
And every where a patty-pack
As if nothing were ominous,
But lions and make-shift girls with ideas

"A real awakening"

I'm not like the people on commercials
Wishing they were celebutards
Even Zack moved past "Punked"
I don't drink to celebrate
Life for so long has been a course right jaw breaker
Of sorts,
As I said, I don't drink to celebrate
Deals or anything splendor as grass
I'm a starving, talented artists artist
Who waits and wanders abroad
Cloudy
To forget all the stings of duping
One time I got lost in a dream
To find the door to my company that moved
It wasn't my company I just worked there
I was just considered a coolie
Contrarily, I guess that's why they left me go
And now my co-workers just stare
I feel like convulsing suds in Washer
And I'm not real contractible to anyone or thing in
Continuance
Because in today's society
People take caution first
And so what if I had a contrivance I might just like you
Before the jar
You could jeer me
Before rousing a quiet bed
That's only a routine for sleep
And in that sleep I imagined all the pangs of longing
Caught up to Debbie D in the macadam lot
Who said, "Take my hand Tim, were almost there
I'll guide you"

But this isn't a Raspberry Song about climax
It's what happens so frequent
In real life not dreams the duping upon waking
Preceding a kiss with a coo
Prowess to a waitress named Alison
Can you see the dimension of my dilemma,
Seizing my heart a rootless wold?
Am I living or in a Precambrian state?
Wouldn't like me moving too much to the little middle,
But superstardom helped quell
All the languidness seen in any terrapin
That move so methodically and tetchy
Now maybe I can start a tenet
To test alliances
And then lastly drink alone,
Just so someone can say so intermittently,
"What are you waiting for."

Del Louis

"Shunning"

He wanted me to play for him
Another restive youth to guide along
And it wasn't just him or her
I shunned along the cumbersome path
Somewhere in pressed time
I didn't figure out the math
Prettier was your hair color
And speckled eyes
All that I missed lining my face still
Trying
To figure out what needs to be done
Even if I mockingly approve of others
Remember how we took me aside
To playfully taunt us in an outdoor gym class
As if I were a leviathan
Pressed against a medicine ball
And I can't get pass
How you enthrall me like a crest to a waterfall
As my mind moves in waves
Contorted like the breezes
On carter's weather vane
Coupled to my denunciation wandering
To doors and latches

"About him"

I wish I had
One memento, even a photo
Of Jack's memory
To mesh, blend into the life
Of all beats in our new millennium
If just for one month
To stay rootless and festive
To the prop of gatherers and one night stands
That sprout from seeds
And the jonquil scented eclectic strangers
I took home to a family
Mired by their own servitude

"Leading to"

We pushed thru
Slanted time
And all I couldn't figure on
Was like this faded 63 nickel
One became negated
To a slough mind
Necessities were for
The other kind of beautiful people
All that I had counted on
Was like broken shoreline
With a sepulchral view
Graceless as dead hung body parts
Wary as steps in war time
What I had hardly noblest
Except a nimble pen and kind words from a stranger
Leading to anarchism and all her niceties

For Theresa

"Refining"

Growing up in the seventies
Seems now so uncanny and
Conventional
With inexplicable expression
We learned to do things
Robotically like catching the bus between Cherry
Without being schmaltzy
You knew a scourge was coming
And early on scholars learned
Boring outdated routines
Gave in to skepticism even to our coach Rodgers
Who seemed raro quis at times
Ranting to bring out our best, journalists
Refining the proposed methods of killers
I remember when Kennedy went down
Was there just a scarce shooter, what was
The real scheme or scoop
Of someone on a grassy knoll just a ghost
Boy did that deflate the sails of humanity
Why would someone try to break our nation,
How could they or a lone extremist?
In-between all that and later grades
The Sedlock twins adorned the halls
Walked steps with their skirts inching up

"One self"

How could you stay
With someone who doesn't want you
For so long
Prayed that thigns weren't inane
And then you still encircle
Bearing your own transgression
And all you can't trammel
Where is your sense of pride, pride, pride
Even in the sepia shades of fall
Now fixed in senescence
As his thoughts are hidden inside the vellum
With words
And you in a veil of deceit without a code
While he becomes vehemently singular
To the needs of a youngster
Tucked to his heart
And you just find a transient stoop
The kind "Zimmy" rested on momentarily
When things become stodgy
Working on a stratagem
Knowing all escape is short lived as love
And every pricked thorned rose
That leads without principle
Back to one-self
So grossly cool
You wanted to creep to your knees
And the pangs of growing pains

Still whipping my mind
Even in this place called Whilom
I feel like I'm doing myself a favor
Breaking a few mores
But stuck behind society's margins
To fight off any mortification
With a fine cluster of friends
Searching for a mountain Laurel's sheen
As time converges us to a single point
That all things are just Judaic
When unchallenged

"Still ringing" (Words) Pt. 2

You tell me about work
How it obstructs weekends
So do grand-kids
And how about the predicable pratfalls
That begin soon enough each Monday
I've had the same dull feelings
That predicate our free time
The bigger delusion: I didn't tell you
Is not having a lass who nurtures
Dread
When you feel you lapsing further down
Because too much conformity killed "Gonzo"
It's like being shackled
To an opaque tree blocking light
When all that was needed was a hand
You came out of the conflagration
Thieves and beggars waited nearby
With a message they embolden
Find the empirical dream
Someone might be waiting for your urging
To sort through the baggage
To unknown worlds
With bigger captions than Broadway

"After were gone"

What are people centers
After were gone
Reality often strange enough
Weird as unsent letters
Stores memory sits like canned shelved goods
Some sweet as candied yams
To see beyond what's left
After were dead, gone
Or jilted without exceedance for some
The happy relations wilted
Untied their strings to something else
Whilst we both expropriated each other
And then we met again briefly, barely
Encountering nothing familiar but folksy whims
You showed me where you moved in Boyertown
The loft you gently climbed on- Wow!
And all I can't remember now
Seems an epitaph for the languid or moist leaves
That flicker on sidewalks or grass
Obtusely and longitudinal from light winds
As if they hid a toad's heartbeat
Underneath their weight
And even after one of us is gone
The other might not ever know
What the world tells us never right
Better left to unspoken virtue
Or the naught of nature so pending

We know less about
Except for quackery scientists and
Meteorologists
Cantor still is cool and efficient
Maybe you already knew
After I'm gone
I might be the candle's penumbra
And guard around y ou
One filled with ebullience
Arching with a slow continuous relaxed ebb
Dancing with a swagger
Until a wistful morning
Made me a vagrant hire
To a vademecum on loneliness
With it's quandaries to fill each vacuities
To a uxorious devotion, Angels wept
Before you left
You wrote in the folio, all that I should do
On page 2

"A staid young grandmom"

Without one innuendo
You keep thought buried
With insentience
As if you're an insole
And I'm not inquisitive
To find what's operative
My mind dreamily traipsed through
Planted seed in wrongful belly
Just to transcend pain
As the vane pointed west
The start of another transcript
One without the felled tragedienne
Of an Eastwood movie
Behind me
Just the amicable stare
Of a quiltess stifled by the design
A ruffled feathered owl
She sat smiling, but wretched
On a porch
Triturating her knees together
Suddenly forgetting how staid she'd become
Doing a strip-tease in a shimmery
Slip and those Astaire slippers
Before the pine trees
And their triceratops branches
Bow in dismay

"Shamed"

How can you
Love so sparsely like partially
Waiting, begging, carrying surcharge
Ready for someone to draw a circle
In the sand
Over all of us and Jerusalem
And this lighted sword
Among the blind non-believers
Fumbling for pieces of Gold
While the real truth has no relic
He marked his spot
And returned to the apologetic flock
As the shepherd sang "Sweet Home Alabama"

"These words"

His words
And mine
Reverberating at 2:19 am
From phone talk
Connected to thin sheaths of cable
It's as if sometimes were answering nothing
But questions to a contest
And I detest Meredith on
"Who wants to be a millionaire"
Are you kidding me with games
Game-man ships are left on fields of dreams
Without ridicule
Unless you're the hapless Sixers
We talk little of ribaldry now that were older
Jenny McCarthy say's rhetorically
Our privates become soft as noodles over time
Time to press on a cigarette as if texting
Some of these words;
True and harsh as an unneeded Savory beating
That ends quickly
When you say, "What if about tomorrow,
And is this what I really want
And in "The Meaning of Life"
Who ate the salmon mousse
What happens when the fervor of courtship wanes?
I might be personally feel more feeble
Than if I let her be

These words telling us about the infinity of a world
Never changing
As if it's closing in a constant pattern
Of Lego pieces made of plastic
Even from the beginning
All these inexorable languish thoughts
We can't escape
It is easier to know the smaller things
When we've overgrown a suitable life
But maybe I can nurture your suggestion
Flux capacitor is playing locally

"To the birds"

To resist graying matter
Is to lose life's enduring visage
The fuzzy back insect
Buzzing by a cutely judgmental
Be as intact without whiffing
As he furiously has always been
Guarding his militia and honeycomb
Know with masterful glee
From time to time
That you can build on ash or loss
As if it had a dew point
Rise above deprivation, the havoc
And all the naysayers
The way you always do
Quicken the haste of longing...
There are other girls with hazel eyes
Even the fervid one
With the gray fichu that fidgets
The way I do
In a slavish winter
Watching the herd of cygnets
Craning to sense
Below the horizon
Mincing all the beauty

"Ever present fear"

In present time we don't live on our terms
In planet terror erred in depression
Fear precedes terminal violence
And then the further roar of pain or gun-fire
Spitting blood and intestines
Roped in the air like tied worms
Slash the tainted air
Without anyone intercepted by intergalactic foes
To take us a board
That would be jaw-dropping to sidled Jihadists
Now camping in Germany
All that fiction purports
Could happen here
And the words carved in ole' hickory, saying,
"All that's tangent and indelible lies in Israel"

"The best and worse of"

The worst thing I ever did
Was keep potential cemented
The best thing I ever did;
Was to wait for serendipity in this narcissistic world
Even if it never comes to light
And also the deed so methodical as line backers pressing
To the thralldom helping the sick
I've done things deemed illogical,
But I'm not like the rest, tjhey still seem logical
As naked prancing chambermaids
I've never dressed up failing
Is not striving
To sustain one's own purpose or bid
The best thing I still did was listen
To thrash or ballads like "Angie"
When I was hurting I needed disassociation
The best thing I ever did and the worst
Was not ever knowing how my memory
Even in silence sustains you
And I am bent like the thistle own in early summer
With the frugality of a furrowed thrush
Contiguous only to the ground or untrimmed willows
Gleaming to some creator

"Before dozing"

Passionate men
The ones you see in forest or gardens
They usually write about passion and loss
But as a care taker of children, instead
I browsed a book Lisa brought to the house before
Dozing
Copyrighted in the UK
About castles and their creepy fascination
Was more thorough than biblical script
I like the Introduction the most
Under the heading of Trades and Skills
I learned the will of the Ale Conner (taster)
Who sat on poured beer staining a bench
With trousers pulled below ass
If his leather britches didn't stick to the bench after one-half
Yeomen, he passed the test
He failed if the beer was too sugary it glued him to the seat
We'll dwell on that shortly about his punishment
When he's taken to the pillory
In the Introduction! About castles
I saw with arrows pointed to the purposeful draw bridge
Raised when threatened turned to reveal a moat
That's where illegals should douse with piranhas
And those strong oak portcullis looked so barbarous
A grille covered by beaten iron that was fire proof
Under the heading weapons and punishment:
The Ale Conner, had his fingertips confined in a finger pillory
After kneeling down in front of this contrampment

Luckily the fellow wasn't skunk drunk
And if a prisoner didn't admit / or deny his guilt
My, oh, my, he got the pressing,
By laying strapped under a thick oak board
As torturers added more weights daily
Many a prisoner wished, begged to be crushed by visitors
Who'd jump on the boards
Less painful than the laws of Istanbul,
Ah, the beauty of intricate castles
Where severed heads could be lined up as soccer balls
These castles filled with armaments
Not only deisgned for
Fun, food and entertainment
Wary a lord who wasn't king
In a Feudal system
Where most were little better than
Slaves or beggars
The way it still is today Johnny!

"Save me"

Random sleek spinster
Like silky washing rain
Save me from ruin
And my shattered self
Dispense all you have
That's resplendent
Rejoice in our combinant nature
Somehow before resurrection
When all that was concealed as dulling
Finish
Repel the safeguard and disconnect
Of not knowing
What tomorrow's bend will be
Just as trustworthy and more
Don't let me fall from a few enamored
Ideas
Let me see the way you save me
From quantum bouts so sedentary
When we held hands
And walked the planes
Before smoothing our souls
Over worn specked rails
Before a sensuous tackle in the snow
The air flitted over a seraph chiming

"2000 miles"

As we got to the door
So prolific to sentiment
As if we o'b'd on tryptophan

"When you gave up"

When did you realize
Nothing matters
Your heart became a sharpened arrow
Saw that it could needle stone
And then you gave up on me completely
And I related to another entity
A long time ago you gave up on us
And I related to others
Now you can't even tell me
A funny remorse joke
As you stroke the feathers on your arrows
Like you were trying to simulate Dietrich;
I'll be gone, no wishes, no good bye's
To this ending
The Jewish author was relatively right
Until that someone makes time stand still
And now it seems it was predestined to a past

"My awakening"

You left me soulless
Sluggard
And fiercely bound
Like a heel on a cursory crag, scuffing his innards
But know I am a sophist
Cast your defiance and I'll rebuke
Before awakening
Built a system so recombinant to immunity
Emerged from a mist of your hatred
Strongly efficient my place on earth
Returning to consciousness
A sorted awakening snoop

"Embracing"

When it is over
After all, come on mellow one
Some walk in a faltering sea without love
Some embrace what's around them
Prey to it's sequence or turbulence
When relations end
Somebody else sometimes dies
Or feels numb
But I can see pas tmy thumb
Dwiddle le do, dwiddle le day-may need
Relish in the odds when there's hope
To know it's 3-to-1 for me

"how I remember carol"

How I remember
Your quiet reserve
Like wild flowers
Standing on a hill
Resisting
Weather's assault
And still you s hook pom-poms
In blue and white
You were so happy
I didn't paw you on a plutonic date
Saw you years later
The same way in "Touch of Glass"
You didn't even know
I liked you

All I know was what your girl-friend
Said so funny
How her mom cleared the ice
Off the car windows at nineteen
I've often wondered how we would've been
Did we have any particulars in common
I still love eating batter dipped fish
I say Mary Ellen,
Recently her walks stopped now
I didn't even ask, about "Carol"
And how I wished I'd remember more
Then talking
As the dawning of time still splinters memory

"Recoil"

To recoil my youth
Not a disobedience to who we are
Caught Charly
In a scrupulous jest
Of hugs and kisses were delighted in
Now just appears
Like wind blowing, curling in a bag
Surely something became transcendental
The softness of her voice lags
Between my ears
Never trailing far
Steers me to variegated rainbows
Before declination
Make me your muse and vehicle
Hide me in your skin miss
And we'll vaunt over drinks
Never tell a soul
All that you can lengthen
When I levitate past drowning
Who'd understand the misinterpretation
That aging
Doesn't have to be fixed misery
Of any kind
When your in my reflection

"Perfection"

The mastery of perfection
As if were striving for even sweeter crumbs
So messianic and numbing
It's kinship effect the likeness to
The mastery of perfection, with
The rhythmic hypnotic chant of "Tumbling Dice"
Timing that's unparalleled, the bass line
At the one minute and a half mark of those grooves
Unmasking greatness that' s not inclusive
And Courtney's vocals on "For Once In Your Life"
Who hasn't felt to ghostly struck
And still lionhearted as we reel
More to life's involution
Hoping for irradiation
While perfection merely has no duration
And can be shattered in a moment's notice
After Zenyatta had gone 19 for 19

"Tallying"

Across barren roads so ragged
Where dry grass and weedy growth
Unsnarls thought
It looks like strangulated seaweed
Marks my mind
With the brevity many have showed me
Staring at nature lapsing
Not knowing where I'm going
Is just as startling
As why I left
Your love die so miniscule
In the hands of lesser men, ….
Who tallied to
The reputation you once had
Still remains quixotic to this day

"Bet willingly"

This illusion of life so improper (Bubba)
And vaguely magical, ever so bold
Hard to grasp
Or what's a valid protocol
To the running lines
Timely clasped as Houdini was
Tried to live the dream of Fitzgerald
Then I found I needed a vent
To vacillate all that's balding
Took to another course (KKR)
Only found Little Red Riding Hood
And vagrancy
To you I was so uxorious
Thinner is a life- that should've been
Three-fold to a better
Still thriving big money and bail-out continues
And all I got was thrusting
Timothy Geinther, look what you've done
With no one to shoulder the blame
Not even a President
Will I someday call you both savior?
Things mostly stayed the same
Maybe I've become squalid as all the others
Someone save me from the knotted link
Literally some have lost the will to think
Mine, the will to conquer most anything
Pulled me from the supple timidity
How we have so much to share
Never thought I'd find a sure fire gal
Even more imposing in front of light and timber
And I swear for once I'm more enthralled
Than any East ender, like a tucked veil below my belly, making
    the next (three) right

"All I could do"

All I could foretell
Like taste without tasting
Hops drying in a warm air
Sweet as when Scarlett Jo enters the room
Why, why, even try today
I could meet some culmination
Toward something other than her hand shake
Or complete loss
The kind that revokes the senses
Better to be a sedentary Buddhist
To let things be in sect
As the seedling over an expanse
Looms and grows
I become more calmly sedate
For what is it to render
To be piquant from afar
Without one placated word of witticism
As if intended love was unholy
Bound to a slip-shod soul
If I'm not more perceptive
Then all I could do was nothing

"Forgotten"

You were just a bit flashy and gangly
Rangy with skin like willow leaves
Cluttering a front lawn
Laid with you on a thin pillow
Til your libido became gamely and tested later
Now it's easier to be resting alone
Standing like the rare birch does in exigency
Effected by the process of aging as I
I'm trapped in the soul of a demoiselle
Did you ever think what this quiet deriding would do
I can still see this description so whorey
From some thirty years ago
Stuck in this vignette and couldn't let go completely
Can't you see I'm strewn to the easel
And all I've heard in mock earnestness
Was how you use to date me
Sooner or later all relations become tedious as random bell
Charts
And somehow I bet I'm still forgotten
And your still basting in ramification of denial
Didn't you know even once
What we had was so rare
Forgotten all those hurrah looks
Forgotten is all that comraderie
With a forgotten huzzah
You don't know what you meant to me ever
Even that Don said you got fuller

"The Wary Truth"

Insane studies
Have led to frugal validation
In our viewed perception of objects, things
As if we the unknown subject
For scientists betwitzed by replicability
When neural drugs let all fail to sustain their
Over time
Even by half
Like ballplayers with diminished returns
Does that mean five aspiring are better than two?
I wouldn't risk the underlying effect
As I'm growing older
Is their anything we can measure reasonably to
Except violence and divorce or foreclosures
With the memories like "verbal overshadowing"
Lest we not forget the failings of random tests
Who are we but ourselves
To try putting, pinning nature to a question
Is like holding down
The obvious elusive quality of a beautiful woman
Who curiously wanders form her man, whispering insatiably
Needing different answers and more intrusion
If only all experiements
Had the same results
We wouldn't look to "fluctuating
Asymmetry"
Found in the pages of Playboy
Even twins and the varying effects
Of the Wood' sisters and every blond
Power
Hopeful.

"Protégé and every wannabe'

To live such a lie
As the faltering truth glides worthlessly by
Like cotton clothes on wash lines
The dye in the ink not quite dry
Wrinkle to what I could find and then so transitory
The infrequency of light
Closing in on a teacher walking
Who seems so in focus
As if he could never be needled by any hocus-pocus
Occasionally like the birds you see in that straight line of flight
Across Tarrytown
Seemingly are the hoaxer
And the rounder's at Trooper's in rotogravure of "Who's"
And I'm not sure why one called me a stalker
Until Don intervened, "He's not"
And I'm not sure
Of the self-reliant groundhog with a full proof plan
Curiously traipsing to February
Peeking out the way dough rises
And my aim bent on one so transgender
But truly combinant to all
Buried all thought in her variegated blonde hair
Spiking all truth
Despite of being my teacher
Who's committed to be the happy despoiler
Widening her margins
As I fumble through her skin to find some marbling
Erasing every lie

"Listening to"

When all was rigid or gone
Still had Ray, Anthony at 6.10,
And Bonaduce
To listen to
Maybe a river's quell or mainstay Don
Rattling off Judy's text messes,
Something about balloons and their phallic shapes
When what was said,
Just dressing up pain
And not his full ideals
Now time lost not knowing what it is she is looking for
Is the same squalid result were begging to
Temporary debasement before we can enlighten ourselves
Sick as all I've heard before this epoch of arguing sides

"A curve in the knowing road"

Do you remember the life we led
Maybe never fanciful enough
Before the Blackberry sourge
Did we kiss the girls as pretty as rainbow trout, yeah, yeah
With lips that could smother
Their own fires
Saw Elva shortly after graduation, working at K-mart
Then she disappeared somewhere askew
And a cheerleader from the seventies
What did she aspire to, one
Looked like Hepburn in that yearbook
So we all took the journey like Eve
Fell sacred to our own star magnitude
Are we more lonely forging to fifty-plus
Because we weren't that way when we had nothing
Except basic structure with little divide
Liked ping-pong, waffle-ball, all the Tapps cards
Without Mantle
Even good perfume burning in the humid air was engulfing
Summers when we were young
Shouldering the truth in our shelters
Now it all seems a blur, weary in a near frozen window
In late December
I took aim at nothing not even my literary agent, waiting
Whilst all that spirituality lurks
Where culture has broken
But the few who stayed are peace to our dissolute island

So happy and thinly bared
Almost finally accepting who I am
In the vein of a Donleavy romp
I seem so in a panic
Until she rates my rigid stem
And goes down farther
Then Miss Thomson had
What's wrong with preying on the heroine
Who wants so little
When I wasn't the full plan, but realities detour
A curve in the road to temporal placidity
Was like those chestnut eyes
That could pierce and read me without one of these words

"Footnotes"

I thought you were well aged
More personable than what I was after
Too hard to petition you from afar
But it's what I do with a raging passion
With a sort of telepathy
That teeters like the homeless
Past tenements in India
Is that too harsh a realism? Without a proper search
Still better to have known you
Than all the termagants abroad
Lastly I can see you through the fluorite in showy glass
Sitting flush without focus to anyone
More viable every flyby in space
Every brief encounter just a leisure footnote
Because I slackened my effort
Of a likely liaison
And footnotes are just mindful reminders
Of every empress or man
Toward legitimacy
Like followed recipes with lemongrass
As I left you with emphatic words
To be stamped and half-paid

"Smoothing over"

On the cross
You made
It's cuts and splinters tear
All of culture's love
Falling out of place
And I couldn't' stay between the seasons
Where habit and routine become a bore
And all I'm faced is an occasional swollen moon
I can't lay in your ruins any more
I can't fill in the decay of a soul that's not solicitous
So I just tried to stay soigné instead
Everywhere I look it still is the same
Except for swoopy shadows from candlelight tilting from air
That smooth my mind and rids this pain

"Following aura"

On this sidewalk
A few leaves become no longer enthralled
Roll past townhouses and inns, travelers
Sheepish like humans in wanderlust
Only scratching to wallop a surface
Trapped by indifference
And it's preponderance
As if by nature I was still in denial's hurtles
Presto I changed to be freed
Like those leaves in autumn scuffling a night's repose
Pretties for you
Pretzel girl
Who enthuses hope
Who enthuses me the most
Above a wonderful hyacinth sky

"Following aura"

The method of your madness, I can't fully restrain
Lies dormant as bricks and waggish like waiting vultures
Hanging on by their weak claws
One a rural weather vane
Never thought you'd be traitorous to all I gave
Would've been vox populi to most
But… then you still descend ravenously on all my triglycerides
Before I shed a skin to leave
To hear a houseful of response planted now, after years
With a posse of followers
I'd call yea women, every eclectic muse
I woo past their disorders and naïf way
To a font of belief and love

"That rush"

I use to get the rush
When we were parted
From my mind's mindfulness and my sex
To come back like geese do
To a warmer place of cover
After the errands, after the work
After extreme sport and play
And countless flirtations I make without
Initiation
As you lay helpless to the deed and stain like smooth glass
Bent on corruption, happily on your knees
Where moonlight made white slits
Down your ribs,
All and more I forgot and should've dotted down
Till love was occasional as bits of Hershey
Or as work room studies at Spiderhead
Ridding the subjects of some darkness and pain
Now I don't get the rush or compulsion
To accelerate being sexual
To a life I've trashed
There is no expectation or a dead sea's rush to calm our neurons
Just ghosts of desperation always
When love was on an upswing once
Or diving down like a drone
So stoic in enemy combat, the two of us
Why couldn't we see? There is no expectation
In half-double accommodations
Trapped in that rubber Rubik cube
Until the axis of hearts turn
Suddenly some kind of rapture

"Accruing To"

I shouldn't have to decree from loss
The way a student of Miller does
There should be no decrement
In the youth of my middle years
Should be splendor of grass
Smiles from streaked hair
And grips around unchanged waists
From ones so pretty and modest
But my only test of time isn't love
It is the almighty pen
With no fixed decimal accruement.

"For Barry" (the gamer)

It's funny
How infinitesimal trades
Mock franchises for decades
The trading of Barry Ball to the bay
Is one hard to make ineffable
With staple reminders like stargell
It's hard to sell an institution
Except in our eras of insignia and
Vast capital
Despite his error he still inspires
The hid who stood in the dugout
Beside Mays became one of the king's
Good luck in federal court
Be strong, be wise, be careful
Don't abort the truth in March
Then win and hunt caribou next fall
Hail Barry, hail suave Barry
And don't ever misconstrue
The miscegenation between us
I've learned a long time ago
You can't hearten the hapless
In the youth of my middle years
Relief from helix dreams became real angels
And acted as heat exchanges
Bending and curbing each hellcat
To their own infirmity and sword
I shared
It's hard to look up from my feet

"Telling"

I stayed up until six, with no one
As if I was waiting to dig a ditch
Trying to find the right forte
London spoke in broken English in a dream
Like the three stooges and Asians still do
And I just wanted to yell
Whilst I was forsaken by all
Only Seth Thomas would listen ticking hard
Like crickets racing before kneeling on concrete
With no on to tell hogwash to
A fortuitous morning will arise
Now wrongful recession on Sunday
Except hawkers at the mall

"Callous"

In your detention of sorts
No luxury, no hubris, pure callousness
No compassion for anyone
Not me or your lovely relatives
Not even goony attached
My God
With hearts like goat skin
Jim dexterously asking for a dollar
To spend at Dunkin'
When I'm as downtrodden as the sod
With one man by my side

"Just know"

It would be a lie
To not know
There would be trials in trenches
Diametric to one's growth
As if they were traversing to some
Unknown transmigration
The trapped doors weighted by pain
Past that buried in thick stone
Wedged to every stiff cusp and stifled breaths
Where I lay in partition
From your departure too many nights
Teared by ghastly gibes while I was stewing
Inside
Needing the beauty of your stigma
Even when piercing light gave me hope
Why'd you try to shrunk me
Into your debasement
When I had to live so singularly
Spellbound still to the other side
Don't you know there is some kind of endangerment?
Everywhere
So sorry if I'd come emulsified to another
Still I loved you first and always
Even if you hate me
There is no one else that masters my domain
May our love be the May Day of tomorrow
Glistening in the repose breeze

Where we watched lovers strolling with glee
Knowing ours is tried and not matted
To materialism or gain
Know Angels will spread and choke out your evil
Pray I don't ask them to
Or I will be restfully gone
As God rescues the maudlin in me
Who believes
All suffering is reasonable
How can I rant about the despicable
When they try to defer you
At the last side bar, God
Have some deliberation and ask them
Why they, they who defile all that's good
Meeting a hard judgment
As the dies are cast

"Offspring"

You wont live forever
But something stays
Parts of me still peerless
I see bits of you in my decadent bathroom mirror
But I'll never change
And every face wrinkled by age
Doesn't stop time or a day's dawn
Opening replete without meaning
Rushing and clearing to dusk
But not without the white tusk of a moon approaching
Bouncing off of us like ricocheting love
Until you came along
Smoothing over every peeve
Without resemblance

"Passage"

On the sturdy stretch that doesn't subjugate
Along Morgan Town
Sublime sheds and barns with stripped paint
Mesh along RT 23
And plowed snow treated with fertilizer
Surreal as thorough art displays
Where a few landau and surreys sits along pebbled driveways
I see the solemnity in luring
With it a shared recession
Making us more capable of giving
And what I sacrificed I loved the most
Was my own sense of realism
Some would say warped of course
And loosely bound
To God's will as one

"Little Mention"

When we were young
We were bold enough to think
We could always envision clarity
But it changes like the reasons here
Every restless bard has to be
Just clinging to pieces or fruit halved by falling
Like lovers cleansed by rain
All I can't keep dethroned by the high king
Just enough to get by
But when I lived I wanted to be remembered
By more than picture frame snippets
One I kept soldiers on in my mind
And all you did was tell a friend
A mention of dating
As though I never mattered
So brief and callous that statement
Channeled to what
More mating and buried lies in their shelter
Some sort of resurrection
And still I wanted you

"Blue love's glint"

Your blue love
Gleefully glistening like a blowtorch
With a mushy scent
Brimming over like a smooth river
Lapping before ensconced
By a delighted sea or the image of many pleased wayfarers
Covering me objectively
As if I were a fawning novelty you spend time with
Secreted as morning dew
That can overshadow meaning
When your oblique as the sky's momentum
Your blue love became obsolescent
Finally just perdurable with revising glides over us
Revered as Hollywood's Stella
As if were all just recycle pseudonyms Alex
Peppery as that blue love casting a sweeping damnation

"Spreading Arms"

Evening ceded by a rushing mind
Incisive gargoyles descend overhead
Carved in gray for a flippant morning
Should've been overlays of felt skin
On your unchanged svelte build
You rid me of
To feel so power less
Like the supine dead in placed caskets
You drained me down to the bottom
Where there's nothing
So easy now to just dredge me away
Somehow to
I'll just filter thru to T-
If only in a dream
And those spreading arms concave
Close around me
Like a high-fastball
As if fairy dust is sprayed
From the magic of unknowing
What compels to concession
Is finding concordant love

"Etching memory"

The geese flew over around eight
So vocal and retentively proposing
Sending a message
Some sort of awakening
Begging me to part willfully
As if I was part of their retrieval
They wanted me
But I don't want to return
Even though I'm deliberate as snow
And stay
And you were just a coal colored flanker like Alworth
Flapping in a delineating sky
Sometimes I have your deftness in the kitchen
But when you passed
I became more sullen
Until a toboggan on a hill swayed my mind
As the titmouse ring
The sled spanked the white ground
Like wild clasped and clapping hands
Simulating an act of love

"Mindful sketches"

All that I had nearly gone
Like a soft wind's whisper comes unglued
Escaping time
I could trace some small vague memory then
Trapped by lost sentiment
Of knowing you liked me
Was a magnetism seldom found
I could still trace like seagulls that survey
Small vague memory for nostalgia or gain
How we walked the corridor as if we were one
And how your mom saved a bird in danger
All you say was note worthy then as no
For shared novelettes
These souls seem lost on a sweeping tide's
Rush
Searching for survival
Until the sea is balanced and even

"Completely chaste"

Doesn't the cosmos lurk in lucubration
To know the weight of feeling
It's curse and blessing
In a micro mesh of refinement
Before we regress
It may now seem so middle some vivacious hid
Hid, as I continually meander like beggars do
Understand
I miss you

Del Louis

"an unfinished poem"

Freed myself from worrying about stipends
It was too much to bear
When the economy froze the private sector
While I'm still sucking dirt like worms do
Evil cannibals rose steadfast
With candor can't live in the past
Of what I wanted never secure
Even as I age each learning curve
Needs what Webster's calls stick-to-it-we-ness
As I look to find the steady stern
No one was around me to mentor as equals
As I stared at your crumbling ashes
Still in a Yiddish canister
Below me the yellow birch color of walnuts
Reminding me of young Sara's eyes
That bartender who attended RACC
Truthfully left me with no one to playfully offend
So I drowned myself with burning rye
On the rocks hickory smooth as General Hancock
Searching for someone who sends me

"Revealing"

Outside the dom
And winter's expression
A bleak peering sun like young rutabaga
Holds a reference to you
Even through these gray powdered skies that diffuse
After all this selfless inquietude
Still a love that's more than insentient
Should I be saying K....
Is this all I can preen
Something that always seemed so foreordained
Surely more than a pleasant dream's inrush
As I wall near or upon the shuffling white doves
Fidgeting on Fifth Ave.
Does it all seem so posse without telling
Promised to make you officious a million ways
Do you see me in a kind reflection
Or just as birds in a smooth minuet

"Favorite one"

I saw you again
You were standing as if you were compressing air
Looking fortuitous, full of decorum
Waiting to be sprung
With your arms crossed at Midas
You had me a red sweater I remembered before
I didn't know it was you, still and mulling
Until my car passed thru
The reality of sending some cosmic scenic
Beauty forward
Did you see me? With a look that makes us mute
Or did your eyes take to the skies
Looking for hung passion
And the clipping power it has
Standing on ceremony as if you were in
Incognito
To the world's imputation
And herself

"In desideratum"

I thought I'd let things be
I did, but they echo loudest
In my head
So I write, write, write
Righteous me
Closing in on the truth
Instead unable to prepossess
What a life without you does
And all this gouging to repair
Along the fault lines to witness in
All our weaknesses
Felt the pongs of desperation immense as seas
Even the attacks of panic on occasion
Like rushing water between timber
When I was sitting still
Stemmed to defiant and dignity
Begging for illimitable fame, the kind equines have
Is like asking for acceptance to fail
When every thing else is denied I think of the gelding "Smile Be
    Happy" and lost friends
You dulled my aging colored in some blanks, don't you
And to have the power to weigh clairvoyance
So damaging to live this lie
While the rye suffocates little difference I could make
Or one that's so lasting – alternate

"Your glitter"

This head now plastering in
To shade my mind of full aging
With the help of Harp
But the look in your eyes
Is like the blistering gleam of fresh
Uncut flowers
One's that wait for spring's adornment
And the sheepish perfectible gaze of the sun
Past down like fading embers tiring
Blanketing or exiting my thoughts
Now all these faces but one –
That permeates a languid soul
Like a calm, forceful buzz Emily

"Lastly"

When I see confetti immersing thru our atmosphere
Every piece so simple but complex
As if celebration remains illimitable
Even to every great poet or athlete, celebutard
They eventually become fallible
In the contest of life time only deceives us
We can only imitate ourselves
Sometimes badly when your part Bortner
Remember more than a game without losers
The poster of Pebble Beach
With these long lavish green fairways
That still imbibes me
And arrowheads I stole from loose earth
Chipped along banks above the railroad on Moser
And here we are if only in imagery to others
Without some form of retainment
Is just a mist or condensation drying
I lost all feeling of immediacy
As if following the traits of every Buddha isn't noble
Yet;
Can't ever side with an iconoclast such as Soros seems to be
But there might be something more for steerage before our end
Please tell me
While some might say you stayed like an arthropod
Before being stilted in imago – that final adult stage
Now I must utter the fact
Should've I been more resounding
Would it had mattered?